11-20-03   Alt

D1542903

The Official Pritikin Guide to Restaurant Eating

The Official Pritikin Guide to Restaurant Eating

Nathan Pritikin and Ilene Pritikin

The Bobbs-Merrill Company, Inc.
Indianapolis/New York

Published by The Bobbs-Merrill Co., Inc.
Indianapolis/New York
Manufactured in the United States of America
First Printing
Designed by Jacques Chazaud

Library of Congress Cataloging in Publication Data

Pritikin, Nathan.
  The official Pritikin guide to restaurant eating.

  Includes index.
  1. Reducing diets.   2. Restaurants, lunch rooms, etc.   3. Food habits.
I. Pritikin, Ilene.   II. Title.
RM222.2.P727   1984   613.2'5   83-3853

ISBN 0-672-52773-1

Contents

Foreword

For every person who follows the Pritikin diet and eats mostly at home, there seems to be another person who, whether from necessity or choice, eats in restaurants very frequently. Many of the latter Pritikin followers have expressed a desire for specific guidelines that would enable them to choose appropriate restaurants, select dishes that are prepared in a Pritikin manner, and in general ensure that their eating-out experiences are healthful and pleasant. Those who already follow the Pritikin way of eating will, we hope, find in this book an answer to the uncertainties that sometimes beset the restaurant eater.

There is another group of people to whom the book is addressed: those who eat out frequently and have been assuming that it would therefore be impossible for them to follow the Pritikin diet. These people may be impressed with the principles of the diet but may see no way of avoiding foods they know to be conducive to heart disease and other degenerative diseases, foods which seem impossible to stay away from in restaurant meals. In other words, these people feel that dining out and adhering to the Pritikin diet are incompatible. This book shows otherwise. It tells readers how to eat out in all kinds of restaurants and still follow the Pritikin diet guidelines.

The Official Pritikin Guide to Restaurant Eating thus fills a need that has become apparent from our many conversations over the years with both present and potential Pritikin adherents. We hope that the information in the book will make your restaurant outings both more enjoyable and more healthful.

Nathan Pritikin
Ilene Pritikin

Santa Barbara, California

Acknowledgments

Many people assisted us with suggestions and professional help as we were writing this book, our first restaurant guide.

First of all, we are grateful to the multitudes of Pritikin dieters across the country who have contributed directly or indirectly to the book. Some of them are alumni and staff members of the Longevity Centers and other Pritikin programs; others are converts to the Pritikin way who learned of the diet after reading a previous book on the subject. Many of these vanguard troops have ventured into the wilds of Manhattan, Los Angeles, Houston, and other major American cities, and even overseas, to chart the way for us in restaurants of all kinds, even converting some restaurateurs in the process. The valuable information they have provided has been extremely helpful in the preparation of this guide.
ration of this guide.

Perhaps equally important, these Pritikin dieters have demonstrated, by example, that eating out enjoyably and following the Pritikin guidelines are not mutually exclusive. We are always happy to see how well people can interweave pleasurable and nutritious dining into their busy lifestyles.

Terry Graves did much important groundwork for this book, and continued her stewardship during the writing of the manuscript. She played a large part in helping to bring our dream to a reality. Our avid research assistants—Nan Bronfen, Janet Trent, and Terry Weiner—assisted greatly in the development of the book. We are also grateful to Esther Taylor, who contributed valuable advice as we organized the material for Chapter 7, and to Diane Grabowski, Betty Sheldon, and Nell Taylor, who diligently worked on preparation of the interim and final drafts of the manuscript.

Introduction

*O*ver the last decade, and especially since the founding of the Pritikin Longevity Center in California in 1976, many thousands of people in this country and abroad have significantly altered their lifestyles as a result of facts brought to them in books, articles, and lectures about the Pritikin diet. The diet, a program of dietary reform that avoids the abuses of the affluent Western diet by minimizing foods high in fat and cholesterol and maximizing foods high in complex carbohydrates, has been demonstrated by clinical experience and controlled research studies to substantially reduce risks of heart disease and other degenerative diseases. In addition, it has proven itself to be the diet of choice of many star athletes, including world-class marathon runners, who have found that eating this way gives them maximum endurance and performance potential.

Ordinary people, too, have experienced the invigorating effects of the Pritikin diet. Young adults, young families, middle-aged people, and elderly people whose lives have been altered by these dietary concepts, have discovered that they feel much better, and are much more secure about their future health. (You can read about some of them, in their own words, in Chapter 3.) These people don't mind the small additional effort involved in shopping for their food, preparing meals, and eating out in restaurants a little differently. The information contained in this book should make those eating-out excursions much more enjoyable for Pritikin diet devotees as well as others new to the diet who want to move closer to the Pritikin diet guidelines.

The Pritikin Program involves more than just changing your diet, however. It's a new mind set, an altered attitude toward living. When you follow the Pritikin Program, you also give up your sedentary habits. For instance, when you eat and exercise* the Pritikin way, you won't hesitate to park your car a few blocks from a restaurant. It becomes enjoyable to walk before and after eating, even if the distances involved are half a dozen blocks or so. The diet allows exuberance to replace the logy feeling caused by eating those oil- and fat-rich meals.

For those who want to learn about the diet, and the many others who will enjoy refreshing their acquaintanceship with it, we answer the question first: just what is the Pritikin diet?

---

*Suggested exercise programs are presented in *The Pritikin Promise* (New York: Simon & Schuster, 1983) and *The Pritikin Program for Diet & Exercise* (New York: Grosset & Dunlap, 1979).

The Official Pritikin Guide to Restaurant Eating

1

What Is the
Pritikin Diet?

The Pritikin diet, unlike most other diets, is not specifically designed for weight loss, although this is one of the pleasant side effects in people who weigh more than they should. The Pritikin diet is designed to help you live longer and feel better. It is unique in being a diet that not only offers the healthiest way of eating but allows you to maintain your ideal weight without restrictions on how much or how often you eat, if you eat the right kinds of foods.

The Pritikin diet is not a faddist or crash diet. It is a safe and sane lifestyle, and, with the exception of dairy products, is based on the kinds of food available to people hundreds of thousands of years ago, when the human digestive and metabolic machinery evolved to its present state.

Today, the typical American diet contains an overabundance of calories and leaves one sluggish, encouraging a sedentary lifestyle. Too many of the calories come from fat and protein, which are inefficient fuel sources and produce toxic by-products. Fat and protein are not as easily converted into actual energy. People mistakenly strive for a high-protein diet because they think lots of protein is needed to keep the body strong. On the contrary, above certain levels protein becomes harmful. A high-protein, high-fat diet is usually also high in cholesterol, and as such has been implicated as the cause of our country's above-average rates of heart trouble, cancer, diabetes, high blood pressure, and other degenerative diseases.

In the Pritikin diet, fat, cholesterol, and protein are restricted to safe levels; the emphasis is on complex-carbohydrate foods. The diet resembles those that people had before the agricultural revolution of the 1800s, when the development of more efficient agricultural methods greatly increased the availability of meat and dairy products. Then, in 1870, the roller mill was invented for the high-speed separation of bran from the starch and protein of grains. In this process, large quantities of vitamins, minerals, fiber, and essential fatty acids are lost; and so bread, the "staff of life" for millennia, no longer provided these essential nutrients. With increasing prosperity, the American middle class, and eventually almost the entire population, had access to foods that in earlier times were available only to royalty and the rich.

Thus, for more than a century, Americans have been steadily and insidiously consuming more meat and dairy products. They have, in short, gradually changed their eating habits from a high-carbohydrate, low-fat diet to a low-carbohydrate diet in which about half the calories come from fat. On top of this, almost all the carbohydrates that Americans consume are derived from refined white flour, which lacks germ, bran, and fiber as well as many essential vitamins and minerals. Worse still are carbohydrates that come from refined sugar, an even more highly processed form of carbohydrate. The average American's diet also contains about 600 mg of cholesterol per day, which in such excess is the major factor contributing to arterial blockage and a gradual choking off of circulation to the heart.

Primitive peoples and other peoples in some of the developing countries have never made this change. And many epidemiological studies have shown that they do not suffer from the degenerative diseases so common in the Western world today. The appendix at the end of this book includes a more detailed discussion of the links that have been established between degenerative diseases and the American diet.

What Foods Are Recommended on the Pritikin Diet?

A varied diet, made up primarily of unrefined foods, will meet your nutritional needs more than adequately. On the Pritikin diet you will have as much fat, carbohydrate, and protein as you need, as well as generous quantities of vitamins, minerals, trace elements, and fiber. And you will not overdo cholesterol, fats, sugars, and salt, which are the main culprits in several degenerative disease processes.

The regular, or maintenance, Pritikin diet allows for 8–12% of calories as fat, 12–15% as protein, 80% as carbohydrates, and a maximum of 100 mg of cholesterol daily. (This is in contrast to the diet of most Americans today, in which fat comprises almost half the caloric intake.) Carbohydrates form the bulk of the diet, and are consumed mostly in the form of complex carbohydrates that come from such foods as fruits, vegetables, whole grains, and beans. The recommended foods are eaten either raw or lightly processed, which means that needed vitamins and minerals are retained. Cholesterol intake is kept down to a maximum of 100 mg per day by a restriction of the intake of cholesterol-bearing foods—meats, poultry, seafood, and dairy foods.

People who wish to lose weight can follow 700-, 850-, 1,000- or 1,200-calorie versions of the Pritikin diet which emphasize the lower-calorie acceptable foods. Low-calorie adaptations of the regular Pritikin diet are outlined in *The Pritikin Permanent Weight-Loss Manual.**

At the Pritikin Centers where participants are medically supervised in a residential program for a minimum of two weeks,† a special therapeutic Pritikin diet is used for patients with degenerative diseases—mainly cardiovascular diseases, diabetes, and hypertension. The diet is much the same as the regular Pritikin diet, except that the weekly allotment of meat, fish, or poultry is under 3 ounces in order to keep cholesterol intake below 25 mg per day. The proportions of carbohydrates, fat, and protein remain the same.

In this book and others on the Pritikin program the regular Pritikin diet is presented.

The most important factor to control in following the Pritikin diet is your intake of cholesterol. Animal products—poultry, seafood, or meat—should be restricted to a total of about 3½ ounces per day, and unskimmed dairy products should be avoided completely. (See chart on pages 15–18 showing the cholesterol content of these foods.) Besides being high in cholesterol, animal products also contain more fat than most plant foods, and, in the typical American diet, they supply more protein than the body needs. On the Pritikin diet, dairy foods, which in unskimmed form are very high in both cholesterol and fat, are eaten only in their skimmed-milk form. (Skimming can remove virtually all the fat and cholesterol.) Even then, because of their high protein content, dairy foods are restricted to 2 glasses of nonfat milk per day, or an equivalent amount of other skimmed-milk products. The importance of limiting cholesterol, fat, and protein is further discussed in the appendix at the end of this book.

---

*New York: Grosset & Dunlap, 1981. (Appreciation is expressed to Grosset & Dunlap for inclusion in this book of selected materials from books published by them on the Pritikin Program.)

†For further information about the residential Pritikin programs, please write to: Pritikin Programs, P.O. Box 5335, Santa Barbara, CA 93108.

On the Pritikin diet, a small amount of alcohol is allowed in the form of a glass of beer or dinner wine a few times a week. Wine is also used in cooking because after a few minutes the alcohol cooks off and nothing remains but the flavor and a small amount of sugar.

On the Pritikin diet, we recommend limiting sodium intake to 1,200–1,600 mg per day. (Some individuals with medical problems such as congestive heart failure, severe high blood pressure, or severe arthritis may need to restrict their sodium intake even further.) All foods contain some sodium naturally, so even if food products high in sodium were totally eliminated from the diet, a person would still ingest an average of 400–600 mg of sodium per day. In order to keep total daily sodium intake below 1,600 mg, therefore, no more than 1,000 mg of sodium per day should be consumed from food products to which salt has been added, such as the ones listed in the chart on page 19.

Table salt or other sodium-containing compounds need to be limited because a diet containing high amounts of salt (and especially fat) has been linked to the development of high blood pressure. Indeed, the incidence of blood pressure problems at increasingly young ages is undoubtedly related to the typical American diet, which is so high in both fat and salt.*

As will be discussed in the next chapter, complex carbohydrates are preferred over simple carbohydrates (sugars) on the Pritikin diet. To limit simple carbohydrate intake, sugar sources are restricted. Fruits, which contain simple sugars, can be eaten in large but not unlimited amounts. Sugars as contained in unsweetened juices are used in small amounts for sweetening, in preference to refined white sugar, brown sugar, fructose, honey, or molasses. Foods containing preservatives are generally avoided because some of them are known to be harmful and the long-term effects of others are not yet established.

An easy way to keep your priorities in perspective when making choices is to remember the following list. The substances are arranged in descending order of harmfulness: that is, cholesterol when eaten in excess is the worst for you, fat is somewhat less harmful, and so on.

---

*Detailed discussions of the mechanisms by which the body is damaged by large amounts of salt, fat, cholesterol, protein, and sugar in the diet, can be found in *The Pritikin Promise: 28 Days to a Longer, Healthier Life* (New York: Simon & Schuster, 1983). (Appreciation is expressed to Simon & Schuster for inclusion in this book of selected materials from *The Pritikin Promise*.)

Priority List of Restricted
Food Substances

Cholesterol
Fat (animal fat and vegetable oils)
Protein
Alcohol
Salt and other sodium-containing
    substances
Sugar
Most preservatives

Bear in mind that the above list is necessarily over-generalized. For example, a lot of alcohol is certainly worse than a very small amount of fat. The list simply provides a convenient rule of thumb: common sense must come into play as you make daily decisions to eat or not to eat certain foods. More detailed guidelines for the Pritikin diet are presented on pages 6–19.

To help you to visualize the diet, let's imagine how your plate would look if you were following the Pritikin guidelines. Instead of a huge steak or several pieces of fried chicken dominating it, your plate would contain a small piece of fish, poultry, or meat accompanied by much larger portions of complex-carbohydrate items. The Pritikin diner often selects dishes such as pasta topped with a sauce made with a little meat or with a marinara vegetarian sauce, or stews with lots of vegetables and potatoes and small amounts of chicken or fish.

Some people have the misconception that a diet which restricts fat, cholesterol, and protein is dull. On the contrary, the Pritikin diet is enjoyed by many gourmets and gourmands. The natural flavors of foods used in the diet have an almost infinite variety of subtle tastes, colors, textures, and aromas. Pritikin meals can be delicious because the cook learns to enhance foods rather than alter them. No gourmet need turn away from the Pritikin guidelines.

Recommended Eating Times

Eating three times a day is adequate, but some people prefer to eat smaller amounts more frequently, having several snacks during the day. Or you can make like a chimp and chew contentedly on appropriate foods from the time you get up until you go to bed.

If you don't eat often enough (or don't eat as much food at a sitting as you need), your blood sugar will drop, causing you to feel hungry and tire easily. Infrequent eating can lead to weight gain, in that people who eat less than three or four meals a day have a tendency to eat more at the next meal, often more than making up for the skipped meal. Further, studies have shown that even if people eat the same amount of food, they gain more weight if they eat it at less frequent, larger meals than when it is divided into smaller, more frequent feedings. So nibbling may be less conducive to becoming overweight.

Studies have also shown a reduced incidence of heart disease among people who eat more frequently than among those who adhere to a three-squares-a-day regimen. In addition, the requirement for protein is significantly lower when the frequency of eating is increased.

Because of the advantages of eating less food more often, when you're eating in restaurants, at times you might choose not to order from the entrée section of the dinner menu. Instead, you might choose an appetizer, side dish, soup, or salad. Of course, avoid the fried appetizers, cream soups, and so on. (See the discussion of cooking methods on page 9.)

Excellent choices can often be found among the side orders. A baked potato is delicious plain, but you might alternatively ask for salsa, which is available in many restaurants, to put on it. (See our discussion of Mexican dishes, pages 63–65.) Other choices would be steamed vegetables, sliced tomatoes, rice, or steamed corn tortillas. A sandwich makes a nice meal, and if you don't finish it, you can ask the waiter to wrap half of it to carry out for a later snack.

Guidelines to the Pritikin Diet

People who follow the Pritikin diet regularly need not concern themselves with obtaining enough nutrients of any kind, including the various vitamins and minerals. They obtain far and above the amount they need. Therefore, for people who occasionally dine out, their primary concern should be to avoid those food fractions that, consumed in excess, contribute to poor health, especially fats and cholesterol. If you get sufficient vitamins, minerals, and fiber, that's great, but if they're lacking in the restaurant fare you order, it doesn't matter, if you eat out only infrequently.

There are some people, however, who eat virtually all their meals in restaurants. They need to take extra care that they are eating a diet that fills all their nutritional needs by making sure they are getting enough of the various food groups that supply such nutrients as the B vitamins, vitamins A and C, iron, calcium, and fiber.

The guidelines to the Pritikin diet (pages 7–8) are intended to keep you on course so that you regularly consume sufficient quantities of the necessary food groups. That will provide you with an adequate intake of nutrients, including the B vitamins, vitamins A and C, iron, calcium, and fiber.

Guidelines 1 and 3 may prove a little difficult to adhere to if you are a chronic restaurant diner eating in restaurants that don't serve whole grains, whole-grain products, or fresh fruits. But the remedy is simple. To make sure you eat two or more kinds of whole grain daily, you can purchase some good quality whole-grain bread, whole-rye crackers, and, if you like, some old-fashioned rolled oats, which can be eaten dry and uncooked. Surprisingly, uncooked rolled oats, sprinkled with a little cinnamon if you wish, can be a wonderful snack food. Make sure the bread and crackers are free of fats or oils. Also purchase some fresh fruit, such as apples, pears, oranges, bananas, or grapes. No refrigeration is required for short periods of storage.

Use the bread, crackers, oats, and fruit for snacking, to supplement your restaurant meals. You can keep your food cache in your car, motel room, or suitcase, if you are traveling.

Keep in mind the guideline information, and adhere carefully to the Do's and Don'ts of the "Table of Foods to Use and to Avoid" (pages 10–14) and to the rules that follow. We'll go into detail on how and what to order in restaurants in Chapter 4.

1. Eat two or more kinds of whole grain daily (wheat, oats, brown rice, barley, buckwheat, etc.) in the form of cereals, side dishes, pasta, bread, or similar foods.

2. Eat two or more servings of raw-vegetable salad and two or more of raw or cooked green or yellow vegetables daily. Potatoes may be eaten every day.

3. Eat one piece of citrus fruit and up to 3 or 4 fresh-fruit servings daily.

4. Do not use sugar of any kind or honey. When sweeteners are necessary, use pureed fresh fruit or fruit juices.

5. Limit protein from animal sources* as follows:

---

*Vegans, who choose to eat no animal protein at all, may require a supplement of Vitamin B_{12} once every several weeks.

- Up to 24 ounces (raw weight) per week of low-fat, low-cholesterol meat, fish, shellfish, or poultry, with a maximum of 4 ounces (raw weight) per day.*
- Up to 16 ounces (2 glasses) skim milk on vegetarian days and up to 8 ounces (1 glass) per day when full daily allotment of meat, fish, shellfish, or poultry is eaten. (Substitutions of other skim-milk dairy products for milk may be made as shown on page 11.)

6. On vegetarian days, 8 ounces of cooked beans or peas may be substituted for meat, seafood, or poultry. Avoid beans and peas on other days except for small amounts in salads.*

7. If you have constipation problems, add some unprocessed wheat-bran flakes (starting with 1 tablespoon daily) to your cereal, soup, or other foods.

8. Eat 3 full meals daily. Don't go hungry between meals; snacks are encouraged. For snacks, eat fruit (not exceeding daily fruit allotment), vegetables, and raw salad, or whole-grain bread or crackers that are free of oil, fat, added wheat germ, or sweeteners.

9. Flavor with herbs and spices, instead of salt. Keep salt intake minimal.

10. If you need to lose weight, increase vegetables and decrease grains. If you need to gain weight, decrease vegetables and increase grains.

See the chart on pages 15–18 for comparisons of the cholesterol, fat, and calorie content of different types of dairy products, fish, shellfish, poultry, meat, liver, and eggs. Note the differences in content when a low-fat or lean version of a given food is chosen.

We advise that caffeine or caffeine-like substances—including regular tea, chocolate, and cola drinks as well as coffee—be eliminated as much as possible. Caffeine, besides having its well-known effect of generating nervousness and irritability, has been linked to disorders such as fibrocystic breast disease in women. Many people are switching to herb teas for their hot beverage.

---

*Protein intake adds up surprisingly rapidly even when one attempts to limit protein-rich foods (animal-muscle foods, nonfat dairy products, and legumes) while on the diet. Ideally, intake of meat, fish, shellfish, or poultry should be limited to around 16 ounces per week (three vegetarian days per week would accomplish this), instead of the allowable 24 ounces per week.

On the Pritikin diet, the way in which a dish is prepared can be as important as the ingredients from which it is made. For example, a low-fat, low-cholesterol fish filet of appropriate size can be made unsuitable if the chef rolls it in an egg batter and sautés it in oil, rather than using acceptable techniques.

Broiling or oven-cooking (by baking or roasting) should be done without the addition of fats, but flavor may be added by basting with fat-free liquids such as defatted broth, lemon juice, or wine. Grilling without the use of fats is also acceptable. Frying or sautéing in butter, oil, or fat of any kind is never an acceptable method.

Steaming of vegetables is most desirable, since there is minimal loss of nutrients when they are prepared in this manner. If cooking in a liquid medium is preferable for particular dishes, whether vegetables or other foods such as fish or poultry, the liquid should be fat-free, although it can be flavor-enriched with herbs, spices, and lemon juice, or wine. After cooking, no butter or fats should be added, of course. You'll need to ask about the mode of preparation used with many dishes, and to suggest appropriate modifications when possible.

Table of Foods to Use and to Avoid

Category	Foods to Use	Quantity to Use	Foods to Avoid
FATS, OILS	None.		All fats and oils, including butter, margarine, shortening, lard, meat fat, lecithin (as in vegetable spray).
SUGARS	None.		All extracted sugars, including syrups, molasses, fructose, dextrose, sucrose, and honey.
POULTRY, FISH SHELLFISH,[1] MEAT, AND SOYBEANS	Chicken, turkey, Cornish game hen, game birds (white meat preferred; remove skin before cooking).	Limit acceptable poultry, fish, and meat to 3 to 4 oz per day, maximum 1½ lb per week.	Fatty poultry such as duck, goose.
			Fatty fish such as sardines, fish canned in oil, mackerel.
	Lean fish, lobster, squid, and other shellfish.	Lobster, oysters, clams, scallops, or squid: 3½ oz/day (replaces entire daily allotment of poultry, fish, or meat).	Fatty meats such as marbled steaks and pork.
	Lean meat.		Processed meats such as frankfurters and luncheon meats.
		Shrimp or crab, 1¾ oz/day (replaces entire daily allotment of poultry, fish, or meat).	Organ meats: liver, kidneys, hearts, sweetbreads.
	Soybeans and tofu (soybean curd).	Soybeans and tofu: 3½ oz/day (replaces entire daily allotment of poultry, fish, or meat).	Smoked, charbroiled, or barbecued foods.

[1]Our revised recommendations are based on a conservative interpretation of the newest data concerning cholesterol and other possibly atherogenic sterols in shellfish.

Category	Foods to Use	Quantity to Use	Foods to Avoid
EGGS	Egg whites.	7/week maximum. (Raw: 2/week maximum.)	Egg yolks. Fish eggs such as caviar, shad roe.
DAIRY FOODS	Nonfat (skim) milk, nonfat buttermilk (up to 1% fat by weight). (8 oz = 1 serving)		Cream, half-and-half, whole milk, and lowfat milk or products containing or made from them, such as sour cream, lowfat yogurt.
	Nonfat yogurt. (6 oz = 1 serving)		Nondairy substitutes such as creamers, whipped toppings.
	Nonfat (skim) dry milk. (5 T = 1 serving)		Cheeses containing over 1% fat by weight.
	Evaporated skim milk. (4 oz = 1 serving)	2 servings/day (on vegetarian days); 1 serving/day (on other days).	
	100% skim-milk cheese, primarily uncreamed cottage cheese such as hoop cheese or dry curd cottage cheese, or cheeses up to 1% fat by weight. (2 oz = 1 serving)		
	Sapsago (Green) cheese.	1-2 oz/week maximum.	

Category	Foods to Use	Quantity to Use	Foods to Avoid
BEANS, PEAS	All beans and peas (except soybeans).	Limit to 8 oz cooked beans on days when fish, poultry, or meat is not eaten. Avoid on other days except for small amounts in salads or other dishes.	Soybeans and tofu (soybean curd) unless substituted: 3½ oz soybeans or tofu = poultry, seafood or meat allotment.
NUTS, SEEDS	Chestnuts.	Not limited.	All nuts (except chestnuts). All seeds (except in small quantities for seasoning as with spices).
FRUITS[2]	All fresh fruits.	5 servings/day maximum.	Cooked, canned, or frozen fruit with added sugars.
	Unsweetened cooked, canned, pureed, or frozen fruit.	24 oz/week maximum.	Jams, jellies, fruit butters, fruit syrups with added sugars.
	Dried fruit.	1 oz/day maximum.	Fruit juices with added sugars.
	Unsweetened fruit juices.	4 oz/day maximum. (28 oz/week) or 1 oz/day maximum, (7 oz/week).	
	Frozen concentrates, unsweetened.		

[2]If triglycerides are above 125 mg%, eat only fresh fruit in the permitted amount.

Category	Foods to Use	Quantity to Use	Foods to Avoid
VEGETABLES	All vegetables except avocados and olives.	Limit vegetables high in oxalic acid such as spinach, beet leaves, rhubarb, and Swiss chard.	Avocados. Olives.
GRAINS	All whole or lightly milled grains: rice, barley, buckwheat, millet, etc. Breads, cereals, crackers, pasta, tortillas, baked goods, and other grain products without added fats, oils, sugars, or egg yolks.	Unlimited. Limit refined grains and grain products (i.e., with bran and germ removed) such as white flour, white rice, white pasta, etc.	Extracted wheat germ. Grain products made with added fats, oils, sugars, or egg yolks. Bleached white flour; soy flour.
SALT[3]	Salt.	Limit salt intake to 3 to 4 gm per day by eliminating table salt and restricting use of high salt or sodium (Na) foods such as soy sauce, pickles, most condiments, prepared sauces, dressings, canned vegetables and MSG (monosodium glutamate).	Salt from all sources in excess of permitted amount.

[3]Normal salt (sodium) needs are provided by foods in their natural state and additional intake should be kept to a minimum.

Category	Foods to Use	Quantity to Use	Foods to Avoid
CONDIMENTS, SALAD DRESSINGS, SAUCES, GRAVIES, AND SPREADS	Wines for cooking. Natural flavoring extracts. Products without fats, oils, sugars, or egg yolks.	Dry white wine preferred. Moderate use.	Products containing fats, oils, sugars, or egg yolks such as mayonnaise, prepared sandwich spreads, prepared gravies and sauces and most seasoning mixes, salad dressings, catsups, pickle relish, chutney.
DESSERTS OR SNACKS	Dessert and snack items without fats, oils, sugars, or egg yolks.	Plain gelatin (unflavored): 1 oz/week maximum.	Desserts and snack items containing fats, oils, sugars, or egg yolks such as most bakery goods, packaged gelatin desserts and puddings, candy, chocolate, and gum.
BEVERAGES	Mineral water, carbonated water.	Limit varieties with added sodium.	Alcoholic beverages.
			Beverages with caffeine such as coffee, tea, cola drinks, cocoa.
	Nonfat (skim) milk or nonfat buttermilk.	See restrictions under DAIRY FOODS, above.	Decaffeinated coffee.
	Unsweetened fruit juices.	See restrictions under FRUITS, above.	Beverages with added sweeteners such as soft drinks.
	Vegetable juices.	Not limited.	Diet and other soft drinks with artificial sweeteners.
	Red bush or chamomile tea preferred.[+]	2 cups/day.	

[+]Recommendations on herb teas (other than the two given) and coffee substitutes are under study.

Cholesterol and Fat Comparison Chart

Source (100 gm, or 3½ oz)	Cholesterol (mg)	Fat (gm)	Calories	% of Calories in the Form of Fat
Dairy				
Blue cheese	75	28.7	353	73
Butter	219	81.1	717	100
Cheddar cheese	105	33.1	403	74
Cottage cheese, creamed	15	4.5	103	39
Cottage cheese, low-fat (2%)	8	1.9	90	19
Cottage cheese, uncreamed	7	.4	85	4
Milk, whole	14	3.7	64	51
Milk, low-fat	8	1.9	50	35
Milk, nonfat	2	.2	35	5
Parmesan cheese	68	26.0	392	60
Yogurt, whole milk	13	3.3	61	48
Yogurt, low-fat	6	1.6	63	22
Yogurt, nonfat	2	.2	56	3

Source (100 gm, or 3½ oz)		Cholesterol (mg)	Fat (gm)	Calories	% of Calories in the Form of Fat
Fish					
Cod	Raw, meat only	50	.3	76	4
Flounder	Raw, meat only	50	.8	67	11
Haddock	Raw, meat only	60	.1	77	1
Pike	Raw, meat only	87	1.0	88	10
Red snapper	Raw, meat only	39	.2	93	2
Salmon, pink[1]	Raw, meat only	34	3.7	119	28
Sardines	Raw	120	8.6	160	48
Sea bass	Raw, meat only	54	.5	96	5
Sole	Raw, meat only	42	.8	68	11
Swordfish	Raw, meat only	68	4.0	138	26
Trout, brook		55	2.1	101	19
Tuna, water-packed	Drained, solid white	63	.9	126	6

[1]The fat content of salmon varies widely. Some types of salmon have up to 52% of their calories in fat. Even at this higher level, it is considered an acceptable choice for occasional use because of its low cholesterol content.

Source (100 gm, or 3½ oz)		Cholesterol (mg)	Fat (gm)	Calories	% of Calories in the Form of Fat
Shellfish					
Abalone	Raw, meat only	54	.3	49	5
Clams	Raw, meat only	49	1.6	78	19
Crab	Steamed	100	3.0	94	29
Lobster	Raw, meat only	84	1.9	91	19
Oysters	Raw, meat only	50	2.2	90	22
Scallops	Cooked, steamed	52	1.4	112	11
Shrimp	Raw, meat only	160	.8	90	8
Squid	Raw, meat only	42	.9	84	10
Poultry					
Chicken, dark	Roasted, no skin	87	6.5	171	34
Chicken, white	Roasted, no skin	87	4.9	163	27
Turkey, dark	Roasted, no skin	101	8.2	202	37
Turkey, white	Roasted, no skin	76	3.8	175	20

Source (100 gm, or 3½ oz)		Cholesterol (mg)	Fat (gm)	Calories	% of Calories in the Form of Fat
Meat					
Beef, chuck	Braised, lean only	90	9.4	189	45
Beef, flank	Braised, 100% lean	90	7.3	195	34
Beef, lean ground	Broiled, 15% fat by weight	90	15.0	245	55
Beef, round	Braised, lean only	90	6.0	188	29
Lamb, lean	Trimmed	99	7.0	186	34
Lamb, lean leg	Roasted, fat trimmed	99	7.0	184	34
Pork, loin	Roasted, lean only	88	14.1	252	51
Rump roast, good grade	Roasted, lean only	90	9.2	189	44
T-bone steak	Broiled	90	10.2	222	41
Veal, rump and round	Broiled	101	11.2	215	47
Liver and Eggs					
Beef liver	Simmered (estimated)	438	4.5	179	23
Chicken liver	Simmered (estimated)	746	4.4	165	24
Egg yolk[2]		1480	30.6	348	79

[2]The yolk from one large egg has 252 mg of cholesterol.

Sodium Content
of Various Food Products

Food Item	Sodium Content
Asparagus, canned (drained)	280 mg per ½ cup
Beets, canned (drained)	195 mg per ½ cup
Capers	233 mg per tbsp.
Carrots, canned (drained)	175 mg per ½ cup
Celery	50 mg per stalk
Corn, canned (drained)	194 mg per ½ cup
Green beans, canned (drained)	160 mg per ½ cup
Lima beans, canned (drained)	200 mg per ½ cup
Lima beans, frozen	86 mg per ½ cup
Mustard, prepared	65 mg per tsp.
Peas, canned (drained)	200 mg per ½ cup
Peas, frozen	92 mg per ½ cup
Salt (for comparison only—should not be included in diet)	2,132 mg per tsp.
Sauerkraut	878 mg per ½ cup
Soy sauce, regular	358 mg per tsp.
Soy sauce, salt-reduced (Kikkoman brand)	211 mg per tsp.
Tomato juice, low-sodium	4 mg per ½ cup
Tomato juice, regular	437 mg per ½ cup
Tomato paste, regular	524 mg per ½ cup
Tomato paste, without salt	50 mg per ½ cup
Tomato puree	249 mg per ½ cup
Tomatoes, canned (drained)	337 mg per ½ cup

2

The Body's Nutritional Needs: Why the Pritikin Diet Is Healthiest

The Pritikin diet not only limits intake of potentially harmful substances such as fat and cholesterol, but also satisfies all the body's nutritional needs. As will be discussed, a person following the Pritikin diet will consume, virtually automatically, all the vitamins and minerals essential to good health. And the emphasis on starches has its foundation in the way the body metabolizes fats, proteins, and carbohydrates.

Why Are Starches Preferred on the Pritikin Diet?

This question can only be answered intelligently by providing some understanding of how the body works—what it does with the large nutrients—fats, proteins, and carbohydrates, as well as with the small nutrients, or vitamins and minerals.

Starches, the preferred nutrient on the Pritikin diet, and sugars are the two types of carbohydrates. Sugars are called simple carbohydrates, and starches—which are huge molecules of thousands of sugars joined together—are called complex. Carbohydrates are used by the body to provide the energy necessary to carry on the many processes involved in maintaining life. Such energy is needed not only for internal processes, such as digesting our food, but for talking, walking, thinking, breathing, and exercising.

Only small amounts of carbohydrate can be stored in the liver and muscles. This means we need to get plenty of carbohydrates frequently to supply energy for our activities. When we eat mainly whole plant foods, such as fruits, vegetables, grains, and legumes, about 80% of the diet is carbohydrates. The food consumed on such a diet will be primarily in the form of complex carbohydrates (starches), and the dietary fiber content will be high. Starches in food are broken down more slowly and absorbed in a lower part of the intestines than are sugars. The result is that blood-sugar levels remain fairly stable. When the natural fiber is left in food, it acts to stabilize blood sugar to an even greater extent. When blood sugar doesn't go up and down during the day like a yo-yo, periods of fatigue are prevented. A diet high in complex carbohydrates and low in fat is beneficial in both the prevention and the treatment of carbohydrate metabolism disorders, such as reactive hypoglycemia and diabetes.

Another benefit of a diet containing mostly complex carbohydrates is that it almost always causes significant weight loss in anyone at all overweight. Most people erroneously think of starches as fattening. Yet both starches and protein have only 4 calories per gram. *It's fat that makes you fat.* The fat in butter, vegetable oils, mayonnaise, and so forth has 9 calories per gram! So it's not the starchy potato but the sour cream and bacon bits—not the starchy bread but the peanut butter—that make you fat. Fat also makes you lethargic and clogs your arteries. This contributes to the incidence of heart attacks for men in their forties and women in their fifties.

Carbohydrates are the body's most efficiently utilized source of energy. They are broken down without forming toxic waste products (as is the case with protein), and they are converted to energy quickly. It takes the body longer to convert fats to energy, and proteins not only are an inefficient fuel source but, because of the nitrogen waste products released during metabolism, they are dehydrating. A person on a high-protein diet risks kidney damage if he or she does not drink sufficient quantities of water.

Protein is used for energy only when a more appropriate fuel source is lacking. Protein does comprise the major portion of most tissues of the body. However, we require relatively little of this nutrient if the diet supplies enough carbohydrates, because protein is recycled so efficiently. We should eat only about the amount of protein we need each day.

Even though carbohydrates are the most efficient and the preferred source of energy, a relatively small amount of potential energy can be stored as carbohydrate. Most of our potential energy is stored as fat. However, we don't require fat in more than very small amounts. This is because the body's fats come not only from the food we eat but from proteins left over after protein-containing tissues have used what they need, and from carbohydrates and alcohol not used for energy.

Unrefined foods, high in complex carbohydrates, are excellent sources of vitamins, minerals, and essential fatty acids. These nutrients, as well as the large nutrients (carbohydrates, fats, and proteins), occur in unrefined foods in optimal amounts and in good balance. In addition, these foods contain no cholesterol, which in excess, as noted, has been implicated in heart disease and many other pathological conditions.

Vitamin and Mineral Nutriture on the Pritikin Diet

The National Research Council's Food and Nutrition Board has established recommended dietary allowances, or RDAs, for the daily intake of each nutrient in amounts intended to ensure adequate nutrition for men, women, and children of various ages and degrees of activity. The Pritikin diet meets the RDAs and, in many cases, provides nutrients in amounts above these recommendations. Interestingly, a person on the Pritikin diet requires *smaller* amounts of some nutrients than those set forth by the National Research Council. This is because, compared to the average American diet, the Pritikin diet is much lower in nonessential fat. The Pritikin diet is lower in protein, too, and also in calories because of the large amount of noncaloric dietary fiber and water present in foods as grown. When excessive fat, protein, and/or calories are consumed, there is an increased need for several vitamins and minerals, including calcium, vitamin E, and some of the B vitamins. The Pritikin dieter who, for a few days, happens to consume less than the RDA for a given nutrient may not actually need as much of the nutrient as a person on a typical American diet.

Vitamins

Vitamins have been a matter of some concern to Americans since the 1940s, when the first vitamin, vitamin A, was discovered. Vitamins are synthesized by plants, as they are needed to carry on the plant's digestive and other physiological processes. Vitamins usually function by attaching to and activating certain enzymes.

When you follow the Pritikin diet, with all its variety, you will get all the vitamins your body can use and then some. Many people believe that taking extra vitamins, especially B,

C, and E, in the form of supplements will provide additional health benefits. This, however, is simply not the case.

Vitamins of the B family are found in grains from which the bran and germ have not been removed. If most of the cereal products you eat are made from unrefined grains, you will obtain all the B vitamins you need.* The amount you need is proportional to the amount of carbohydrate in the diet. When you eat whole grains, which are a source of both, the more carbohydrate you eat, the more B vitamins you get. An excessive amount of the B vitamins will do more harm than good. For example, too much thiamine can cause allergic-like reactions, and niacin overdosing can cause flushing, headaches, cramps, and nausea.

Humans do not have the ability to make vitamin C, or ascorbic acid, as most animals do. Therefore, some people mistakenly believe they need to take large amounts in the form of supplements. Vitamin supplements not only are uncalled for but are potentially hazardous to your health. Vitamin C facilitates the absorption of iron and calcium, but it inhibits the absorption of vitamin B_{12} and copper. Thus, taking large quantities of vitamin C can cause serious vitamin and mineral imbalances, as can also be the case when taking supplements of other vitamins.

Some people believe that vitamin C is good for heart-disease patients, but because it increases the tendency of the blood to clot, it raises the risk of having a heart attack. It has been claimed that in large amounts vitamin C protects against heart disease by lowering a person's cholesterol and/or triglyceride level. This claim has been disproved.

One of the most prevalent beliefs about vitamin C is that it can prevent the common cold or shorten the duration of a cold you already have. There is some evidence that a regular, modest intake of vitamin C, as contained in the Pritikin diet, is beneficial as compared with a diet abnormally low in vitamin C. However, there is no proof that megadoses are in any way desirable. In fact, instead of helping to prevent colds, large doses for prolonged periods of time can have the opposite effect.

Vitamin C supplementation can even cause scurvy, a disease characterized by spongy gums, loosening of the teeth, and bleeding into the skin and mucous membranes. If you take the vitamin over an extended time, your body becomes conditioned to the dosage and dependent on an abnormally high intake. (This is similar to the phenomenon that occurs with

---

*Vegans eating no animal protein at all may require a supplement of vitamin B_{12} once every several weeks, since plant foods ordinarily have no B_{12}.

drug tolerance.) If you then reduce the dosage to a normal intake, you may experience ascorbic acid deficiency symptoms, or "rebound scurvy," until your body readjusts to its normal state. Many cases of scurvy have been seen in infants. Infantile scurvy can result from an expectant mother's ingestion of only 400 mg of vitamin C a day. Vitamin C can induce menstrual bleeding in pregnant women, and it is thought that high intakes may terminate pregnancy or prevent conception. Therefore, vitamin C supplements should not be taken during pregnancy. Some adults who have taken large amounts of vitamin C become permanently dependent on larger amounts. A normal diet is no longer capable of meeting their needs, and without supplements, they develop scurvy.

In sensitive people, large amounts of vitamin C can precipitate attacks of gout; in others, it can cause oxalates to be excreted in the urine, increasing the chances of kidney-stone formation in susceptible individuals; and in people with other metabolic abnormalities, vitamin C supplementation causes the red blood cells to break down. In at least one such case, the death of a hospitalized patient was due to vitamin C therapy.

On the Pritikin diet, you'll obtain an average of 300 mg of vitamin C a day—five times the RDA, but not enough to be toxic.

Vitamin E, found in most foods, is a complex of fat-soluble substances called tocopherols. Whole grains and leafy greens are especially rich sources. The vitamin combines easily with oxygen, thereby preventing hormones, vitamins, fatty acids, and other substances in the body from being destroyed by becoming oxidized or rancid.

Not long ago, an onslaught of advertising claims led people to believe that vitamin E supplements would make them sexier, keep them from aging or developing heart disease, and give them more stamina and endurance. Each of these claims has been scientifically disproved. Supplementation with vitamin E is less dangerous than with other fat-soluble vitamins, but weakness and fatigue can result from taking large amounts. However, there are very few documented cases of vitamin E deficiency in humans, because vitamin E is so prevalent in common foods. It is stored in tissues throughout the body for long periods of time and is therefore available as needed in the system.

Minerals

The foods we eat also contain minerals. These tiny elements remain in the body after our food has been metabolized, not unlike the ashes left after wood is burned. Maintaining the proper balance of these minerals in the body is extremely important. Minerals help regulate the body's water and acid/base balance; are essential components of hormones, enzymes, vitamins, bones, teeth, hair, nails, and blood and other body fluids; and play a role in the functioning of nerves and muscles. Unprocessed foods are the best source of these minerals. In some segments of our population, however, especially among females, the intake of calcium and iron is marginal. The reasons are that the high-fat, high-protein diet eaten by most Americans creates an increased need for calcium and iron, and that many people avoid eating leafy green vegetables, which are rich sources of these minerals.

If your diet contains a variety of fresh, unprocessed foods and modest amounts of leafy green vegetables, you have no need for mineral supplementation. In fact, taking mineral supplements is potentially more dangerous than taking vitamin supplements. If, for instance, your daily requirement for potassium were taken all at once, you could become quite ill. And many cases of iron poisoning are seen each year in young children who ingest an excess of mineral-vitamin supplements. Selenium poisoning may become common in the near future, because selenium has recently become a popular supplement, and only a little more than the required amount can cause severe symptoms of toxicity in humans and animals.

Children's Special Needs

Children, because they are growing, have a relatively greater need for calories and some nutrients than do adults. Therefore, children's diets should include ample servings of nutritious foods that are higher in calories. These include whole grains and whole-grain bread and pasta; hearty bean soups; starchier vegetables such as white and sweet potatoes, winter squash, and peas; and, for nonvegetarians, small amounts of poached or steamed lean fish, or skinned white meat from chicken. Don't put young children on a low-calorie version of the Pritikin diet—one that emphasizes salads and thin soups, for instance.

It is important to include a wide variety of fruits and vegetables in the diet to ensure an adequate intake of vitamins and minerals. (This applies to adults as well as children.) Leafy green vegetables such as broccoli; Brussels sprouts; kale; collard, mustard, and turnip greens; bok choy; and darker varieties of lettuce are valuable because of the important nutrients they provide. (Spinach, beet greens, and chard should be limited in the diet, since they are high in oxalates, which inhibit the absorption of calcium.) Other good vegetable and fruit choices include carrots, winter squash, sweet potatoes, peas, asparagus, sprouts, cantaloupes, papayas, oranges, and bananas. But don't limit your child or yourself to these particular fruits and vegetables—many others also contribute valuable nutrients.

In addition to nutritious foods, children need regular exposure to sunlight in order to obtain vitamin D. Exposure to outdoor sunlight causes the skin to manufacture this vitamin. Fifteen minutes a day is adequate exposure for fair-skinned children; those with darker skin need slightly longer exposure.

Young children often do not care for fancy dishes with tomatoes and spices, or for combinations of food in such dishes as casseroles. It's usually best to serve them simple foods—plain baked or mashed potatoes, whole-grain cereals, lightly steamed vegetables, and so forth. Offer younger children steamed or baked vegetables such as potatoes, carrots, broccoli, cauliflower, or winter squash, cut in large pieces that they can pick up by hand. Soups are often well accepted by children, especially thick, hearty soups, with ingredients such as barley, split peas, or beans.

On the Pritikin diet, the nutritional needs of people of all ages are met by a well-balanced diet composed predominantly of whole grains, fruits, and vegetables—foods that contain mainly complex carbohydrates. The diet meets the body's needs for protein and fat, supplies sufficient fiber, and provides optimal amounts of the essential vitamins and minerals. Finally, the Pritikin diet reduces the risk of developing heart disease, diabetes, hypertension, and other diseases, because it is low in fats, cholesterol, salt, and refined carbohydrates. It is a diet that will make you feel healthier and more energetic, and that offers a large variety of delicious foods that need never leave you feeling deprived.

3

People's Experiences with the Pritikin Diet

Whatever your age, whatever your state of health, you will benefit from the Pritikin diet. People who thought they were healthy discover to their amazement that they really didn't know what feeling well meant before going on the diet. They are thrilled with their increased vitality and endurance in physical activities. People who haven't been feeling well also gain in vigor and energy, in addition to normalizing blood pressure, blood sugar, and other parameters by which physicians measure our state of health. And for most, weight loss, when desirable, seems to occur on the Pritikin diet without any effort.

The healthful results of the diet have been demonstrated in studies conducted by the Pritikin Research Foundation, a number of which have been published in medical journals. If you are interested in the scientific literature, we will send you reprints of these studies upon request (see "Special Services Available," page 199). Many people, however, are more interested in what people like themselves have to say. For this reason, we have included in this chapter some letters written by individuals who have been on the Pritikin diet. The letters are representative of thousands we've received from people all over the world who've reaped health benefits from the diet.

The first letter is from a woman who, along with her husband, was put on the Pritikin diet because of their high blood levels of cholesterol and triglycerides (fats)—both of which are risk factors for heart disease. Mr. and Mrs. G. not only curtailed the progression of existing cardiovascular disease but lost weight in the process. In addition, Mrs. G. not only likes eating Pritikin food but is enjoying cooking more than ever. She and her husband manage to stick to the diet even though they eat out very often.

November 2, 1980

Gentlemen:

Our doctor recommended that my husband and I go on the Pritikin diet because our cholesterol levels were high and also our triglyceride levels. I suffer from angina (under control) and my husband hypertension, which is also under control.

My husband lost 14 pounds and I lost 10 pounds. We have continued eating on the recommended plan and eat out very often, and by just keeping to the fundamentals of no fat, cholesterol, sugar, or salt, my husband lost 4 more pounds (18 in all). I am a small woman and did not lose any more but have kept to the same weight, the loss of 10 pounds.

We look much better and feel very well. It is 4 months now since we have been on the program. Our doctor is delighted with us.

I am enjoying cooking more than I have in years . . . .

Gratefully,
Mrs. R. G.

The next letter, from Shreveport, Louisiana, is from a woman whose initial reaction to the Pritikin diet was typical of the horror many people experience at the thought of food lacking in fat, cholesterol, sugar, and salt. Like so many others, she too learned to modify her cooking techniques so that the food she prepares is both healthful and pleasing to the palate.

October 28, 1981

Dear Sir:

My doctor put me on the Pritikin diet on May 12. I lost 18 pounds the first month, and as of now, am down 34 pounds. I must remain on this food plan the rest of my life, as I've developed some heart problems. I still have 15 more pounds to lose.

I have appreciated the recipes in your book very much and have learned to adjust some of my recipes also . . . .

Having tried about every diet that was ever developed, you can imagine my chagrin when the doctor said "Pritikin." No salt, no sugar, no caffeine, no fat—but it works!

Thank you in advance for any additional suggestions.

Sincerely,
Mrs. H. A.

The next letter is from a woman who put herself and her family on the diet:

October 1, 1979

Dear Mr. Pritikin:

Thank you! Thank you! When you appeared in our city on May 9th, I was bedridden with cardiac and pulmonary complications of systemic lupus erythematosus. My blood pressure was 212/184, my resting pulse was 126; a walk to the kitchen required a rest stop and a nitroglycerine tablet. My sedimentation rate was quite high, even with Prednisone and Imuran, and I swallowed Tylenol #4 like candy.

On May 10th, with my doctor's permission, I began the Pritikin Program diet and started walking, 250 steps a day. Twenty weeks later, I have lost 49½ pounds, my blood pressure is 140/89, my resting pulse is 76, and my sedimentation rate is down. I walk 3 miles in the morning, 1 mile each evening. I haven't needed a Tylenol #4 in weeks and rarely use a nitroglycerine tablet. My doctor is so pleased with my progress that he has put his father on the Pritikin Program and is recommending it to other patients.

I can't begin to tell you how fine I feel, not just physically but mentally. For the first time in several years, I am thinking positively and I have hope.

My children are 12 and 14. I am interested in a medical opinion on putting them on the diet exclusively. Is the diet adequate in protein, calcium, etc., for growing bodies?*

Again, thanks from myself and from my family, and we hope you will continue to work toward a healthier-life guide for everyone.

Sincerely,
N. S.

Seven months later, N. S. wrote to apologize for not having responded to some questions we asked her about her health. Her excuse was, "I have been so busy enjoying *good health,* I haven't stopped to take the time to bring you up to date." She reported that not only her health but that of her children had improved greatly in the year since she first put her family on the Pritikin diet, and this observation was made by their pediatrician as well.

Two years after going on the diet, N. S. wrote, "My health continues to be good, with the lupus well under control. My doctor checked me last week. He said he couldn't believe how healthy my heart sounded, and he wished he and his medicine could take credit, but that credit was owed to Nathan Pritikin."

---

*This question is addressed on pages 26–27.

In 1983, four years after going on the diet, we received the following letter from N. S.:

Dear Friends,

These smiling faces of my children, Mark and Elizabeth [photo enclosed], are due in large part to the three of you. As you may remember from my past letters, when I started on the Pritikin Program in May of 1979, I was bedridden with heart and lung complications of systemic lupus erythematosus. The doctors had just told us my liver was failing, and they doubted I would live to see my son graduate from the 8th grade at the end of that May. Well, not only did I make that graduation, but I took this picture as we were leaving for Mark's high school graduation this past May.

I am so grateful to Nathan Pritikin for working up his fantastic program, to Ilene Pritikin for devising such delicious recipes, and to Nell Taylor [Nathan's secretary] for her encouragement and friendship via the mails . . . .

So all my family sends many thanks and warm thoughts to all three of you.

Sincerely,
N. S.

The Pritikin books for laypeople are not meant to replace adequate medical attention for serious or even not-so-serious health problems. They are meant for healthy people who want to stay that way and also to feel even better. However, N. S. and her family derived invaluable benefits from eating the Pritikin way. N. S. wisely followed the Pritikin Program under the supervision of her physician.

Healthy people who are overweight lose pounds and gain new energy and stamina when they follow the Pritikin diet. They overcome constipation, they have fewer headaches, they sleep better, and most of them have a drop in their blood pressure. These were the benefits expressed in the following letter to us from Fairfield, Connecticut:

August 12, 1983

Dear Mr. Pritikin:

I don't write many letters, but this one has been gnawing at me to be written for over a year. Here goes—heard you being interviewed by Bob Grant on WMCA in New York one afternoon in late winter of 1982. I think it was the day of the blizzard but do not remember that aspect. I know only that hearing you marked a milestone in my life.

I considered myself reasonably healthy and most observers said I was not fat, though I felt I was too heavy . . . . Suffered hemorrhoids and a serious chronic back pain. Had no stamina, had constipation, poor sleeping habits.

Had tried all the diets named after a major city in the free world, taken diet pills, bought Weight Watchers' dinners. Never stuck to one very long because I did not see any results. My trouble is: I'm a walking garbage compactor—I love to eat, anything, anytime, anywhere. Dinner each evening consisted of large portions of meat and salad (with mayonnaise and ketchup). Skip the potatoes and dessert, they are fattening.

I don't know how heavy I was because I had stopped weighing myself at 180 pounds. Maybe I was 185. You see, I didn't think your system would influence my life any more than the others. So, more out of curiosity I bought your book and started working toward your guidelines. Even before I was fully phased into your program, I noticed one morning that I had pulled in my belt a notch. From that moment on, all doubts were removed and I was a solid convert. I now weigh 142 pounds, height 5'7", and have held there for over a year. I have never felt better. All my aforementioned ailments are gone, I have stamina, energy, feel like 20 again though I'm 54 years old.

Blood pressure was never high, but now when I am being examined to donate a pint, I get comments from the nurse like, "You have the blood pressure of a teenager." For example, a recent testing was 100/70.

Thank you again, Mr. Pritikin, you have contributed greatly to my health personally, and to the betterment of mankind in general.

Your friend,
W. H. T.

The writer of the next letter, Jamie L. Marsden, started with a different situation: she, her husband, and her young daughter were healthy, and she put them on the Pritikin diet to keep them that way. They are pleased not only because of the "health insurance" they took out, but also because of the almost immediate effect on their feelings of well-being.

[Received May 13, 1982]

Dear Mr. Pritikin:

I would like to thank you personally for the work you and your staff have done in the field of nutrition, and for sharing your findings with others. My husband (35), daughter (5), and myself (32) began your program on January 27 of this year and we have never felt better in our lives.

We heard of the program through an acquaintance, and after purchasing and reading your *Pritikin Program for Diet & Exercise,* we plunged headfirst (or should I say stomachfirst?) into your recommended diet. As the cook in our family, I began to eliminate the items in our cabinets and refrigerator which we had always considered OK for our bodies, and started filling them instead with fresh fruit, vegetables, and grains.

Although my husband and I have enjoyed fairly good health, we began to notice the middle-age spread setting in and our energy levels falling. In the past we have tried various popular faddish diets to try to maintain our youthful figures. Until learning about your program, we didn't realize that we could eat well and not gain a pound by simply modifying the types of food we were consuming. It's a great feeling to know that we will not have to face "dieting" in the traditional sense again in our lives if we stick with the Pritikin Program.

Your diet plan works because it is immediately reinforcing. Within only a day or two one can actually *feel* the difference. Because we notice bad side effects if we cheat on the diet, our newly acquired eating habits are beginning to be second-nature. Our friends are astounded as to how someone would voluntarily give up such wonderful things as alcohol, coffee, butter, nuts, cheese, and sweets after reading one simple book. We don't consider it fanaticism in the least. We consider it the only intelligent decision to make when you consider the consequences of the traditional American diet.

All three of us are exercising vigorously daily—we know from experience that this keeps us feeling good and looking good all day. Others have commented frequently about how much better my husband and I look, and they still are left open-mouthed when I tell them I jog 4 or 5 miles a day, do calisthenics, and lift weights. Try doing that on a diet of junk food!

Keep pushing your program on all levels. Once people begin, they will see and feel the difference, and it will be difficult for them to ever return to their old eating habits. If you put regular gas in a car built to run on only ethyl, you have only to drive it a few miles to see that it is not working efficiently—our bodies respond the same way and we are now convinced of it.

The Pritikin Longevity Center is one organization we'd like to see "live" forever. We need more of those in the world who are devoted to the betterment of mankind and fewer of those who would exploit us. Thank you for your contribution to your fellow human beings.

Sincerely,

Jamie and Chris Marsden

The next letter was sent from Australia by a man who adopted the diet to prevent cardiovascular disease. He was already healthy, and his new dietary habits caused him to feel even better.

July 5, 1983

The Pritikin Centre,

Being fit and healthy has always been a fascination of mine, and as a result I try to read as much about the subject as time will allow. Once upon a time I believed that if a person exercised enough aerobically, he or she would avoid modern degenerative diseases. However, from time to time I became more aware that something was amiss. Why should it be that some supposedly very fit and healthy people die at a relatively young age? Well, needless to say I have read *The Pritikin Program for Diet & Exercise* and found my answer . . . .

The thing that amazes me the most, however, is that despite all this documented and logical evidence, why isn't the Pritikin diet better known? If cardiovascular disease is the most prevalent of modern Western man's diseases now, why don't governments and medical authorities promote its use to cut down on the gigantic medical expenses incurred through a simple case of bad diet?

I know personally that the diet works, as I have been on it now for about two months, and I can already feel a difference in my well-being.

Yours sincerely,
Stephen Nixon

And we even received a letter from as far away as the Fiji Islands. K. C. N., like many other people with sleep problems, found the diet helps him to have more restful sleep. Most people also find that they require less sleep and have quite a bit more energy.

[Received June 30, 1980]

Dear Mr. Pritikin:

Hello there in the United States of America. This is away out in the South Pacific, a very small group of islands known as the Fiji Islands. I hope you have heard of it just as we have heard of you out here.

Well, Mr. Miracle, I hope you will receive my letter in a god's spirit.

I am now thanking you for your great plan and programme, which I and my wife are now following, and I found it a great success. I used to get a lot of trouble in sleeping, which our local doctors never cured me of until I followed your plan about 8 weeks ago.

May God bless your great plan and family.

Yours sincerely,
K. C. N.

Letters like this one from a young nurse are especially heartwarming and satisfying, as health professionals are in a position to have a strong influence on the lifestyles of others.

[Received November 8, 1982]

Dear Mr. Pritikin,

I am writing this letter to say how grateful I am for your marvelous program and the terrific recipes. I have read all your books, and have followed your program now for three months.

I am 33 years old, a registered nurse on a medical unit. After seeing all the cases that come into the hospital, I can tremendously appreciate your program and philosophy. I am in good condition, 5′8″, weigh 120 pounds, and have a 15% body fat. I am interested in modeling fashion and cosmetics, and I also do quite a bit of jogging. It's a great feeling to jog and feel my lungs fill up so fully. I know my vital lung capacity has increased. It doesn't do any good to be just concerned with the exterior, and to neglect the internal and spiritual elements. Before reading your book, I ate a lot of junk food and drank coffee. Now, I refer to your guidelines and plan my meals according to them. I have 100% more energy now that I am being fair to my body.

I'm glad I've started this program while I am a young woman. My father died of cardiovascular disease. He fits so many of the letters and histories which you describe . . . .

I have told many doctors and patients and friends about your program. Whenever there's a potluck at the hospital, I take various recipes and items from your book. People love them and can't believe they are without cholesterol, fat, and salt.

I am indeed grateful to you and read and refer to your books daily.

Sincerely,
Mary Jane Rivers, R.N.

Now, a year after she wrote us this letter, Mary Jane still follows the Pritikin diet and enthusiastically encourages her friends and patients to do so too.

Larry West, a physician, is another health professional who is actively and enthusiastically encouraging fellow physicians, patients, and other laypeople to make the same lifestyle changes he did.

November 29, 1982

Dear Nathan,

It is finally time to write you a personal letter. Your books, precepts, and wonderful plans for helping people have been a dominant, exciting force in my life these past 3½ years. Thank you.

Let me explain. The day before a marathon race in May 1979 in Eureka, California, you spoke to the runners. I'll never forget your message: "Unless you watch what you eat, all your fitness may not add up to health." I took it half seriously, doubted it along with Victor Herbert and other authorities. But the first-rate 5th Pritikin Research Foundation Symposium* in Santa Monica in October 1981 convinced me and my wife to stick with it. Now I am known as a local Pritikin agent here, and I'm proud of it. We had a wonderful visit with Steven Zifferblatt[†] for his May 1982 public address where I work. I have given a number of talks for the clinic nurses and physicians, and I continue to extol your program.

About my personal history. Starting at 195 pounds in February 1978, age 39, I resolved to become fit to resolve my back trouble. In 10 months I managed to finish the Hawaii Marathon in 4 hours, 33 minutes, at 172 pounds. More back trouble for 2½ years kept me less active. But I decided to take a positive approach, went to the Santa Monica meeting, and started telling my patients about your program. I too became a patient, dropped my cholesterol from 195 to 148, and regained my late teen weight of 158 pounds. This past summer I ran in our first Olympia Marathon in 4 hours, 6 minutes. And in October in the Portland, Oregon Marathon I broke the 4-hour barrier—3 hours, 56 minutes. Your diet allowed me a reasonable training schedule (30–40 miles per week) rather than the costly one previously (50 miles plus per week), and that certainly made my wife happier.

I look forward to attending the 6th Symposium of the Research Foundation when it happens.*

Again, deeply felt thanks to you. Your ideas amount to my "midlife crisis" change! What a challenge for an M.D.!

Sincerely,
Larry West, M.D.

---

*These conferences are held at irregular times. Continuing education credit can be obtained by physicians and other health professionals for attendance. For information on future conferences, write to: Pritikin Research Foundation, P.O. Box 5335, Santa Barbara, CA 93108.

[†]Dr. Zifferblatt is a health educator at the Pritikin Longevity Center in Santa Monica, California.

The next letter is from a man who feels the Pritikin diet reversed his hardening of the arteries. He and his wife have been on the diet for ten years and have never felt better.

July 6, 1982

Dear Mr. Pritikin:

My wife and I have lived on your diet for the past ten years, the first five on maintenance, the last five on regression* with game pheasant or chicken once or twice a month accompanied with wine. I am 59, my wife 52, and neither of us has had any major illnesses in our lifetime. I have been running for 18 years, and between running and walking have averaged at least 60 miles a week for the past ten years. I ran and finished the New York Marathon in October 1980, and also ran as much as 30 miles on weekends alone. My stress test a year ago convinced my doctor, who is a cardiologist and also a runner, that Nathan Pritikin proves conclusively that hardening of the arteries is reversible. My resting pulse was back to normal in five seconds.

My wife and I look at least 15 years younger than our actual ages and have never felt so wonderful as we do today, thanks to you. My cholesterol level is in the 125–130 range, and my wife's is slightly higher. I am 5′8″ tall and have practically no body fat. I have no extra heartbeats showing on my EKG.

Thank you most sincerely for changing our life patterns and adding innumerable years to our lives.

Sincerely yours,
Richard W. Lawrence

Richard Lawrence still follows the diet almost 100%. In restaurants he usually orders salad, fish, and a baked potato. He says he is "sixty, going on thirty!" and that his energy is boundless.

People who fancy themselves gourmet cooks and people who consider eating to be one of the greatest sources of enjoyment in life often lash out at those who eat Pritikin-style, whether the poor Pritikinites are pushing their views on others or are unobtrusively doing their own thing. Such attacks usually come only from people who feel threatened by the positive beliefs and actions of others—for example, the woman who, on seeing a Pritikinite, feels guilty because she knows she is feeding her family in a manner that does them bodily harm; or the man who, facing his Pritikinite friend

---

*A reference to the therapeutic diet used at the Pritikin Longevity Center (see page 3).

across the table, nevertheless orders his regular lunch: a pastrami sandwich, French fries, and a milkshake. Some cooks fear the loss of the pleasure of preparing fine food, but this is an unwarranted fear. The natural preparation of wholesome and nutritious dishes, whereby the inherent flavors, aromas, and beauty of food are enhanced rather than disguised, is a challenge to the true creativity of a chef. The following letter from a young man in Jerusalem should be an inspiration to many who aspire to develop their culinary skills.

September 7, 1981

Dear Nathan:

Thanks so much for your discoveries and your communication of them. I can feel a lightening up and increased joy from running regularly and eating well. I've actually discovered my ability as a gourmet cook. It's very magical. Everything I've touched in cooking in the last two weeks has turned into gold. I created a dessert the other night which was delicious—slices of fresh oranges and peaches and bananas, as well as some raisins; some creamy nonfat cheese sold in the stores here; and as a final touch, some chestnut puree, which I found on the shelf of a small neighborhood store. Two friends also thought it was terrific.

I'm studying to become a rabbi, in the Reform tradition, and I know it is essential for me to have my body be well and alive. I've been working on my nutritional habits for a couple of years now. When I came to Israel, I put myself on the diet and have truly enjoyed it, and when I've gone off it, I've really felt the cost.

Thanks again for your work. I support you totally. It's a pleasure to acknowledge you. Take care.

Sincerely,
A. D.

The next letter is from a young woman who travels extensively. We first heard from her in a burst of enthusiasm after she had been on the diet for only eight days. Shelley spent three of those days away from home, and managed to dine out successfully.

June 29, 1982

Dear Mr. Pritikin,

This is not your typical dieting success letter. I am not yet glowing with elation over the number of pounds I've lost. The reason: I've only been on your diet, or eating and exercise program, for eight days. I am happy with my five-pound weight loss, but I am elated to have found a prescription for better health and well-being.

I am a 31-year-old woman who has carried around fifteen excess pounds on my short but medium frame for the last twelve years. I have approached my ideal weight for brief periods during the last twelve years, but the weight was regained as quickly as it was lost. I've tried numerous diets and visited unethical doctors who quickly shelled out appetite suppressants, thyroid pills, and diuretics. The worst was one week on the Stillman diet.* After one week I felt ill and weak. I felt as though I was poisoning myself. When I was taking drugs and when I was consuming mass quantities of fat, I knew it was all wrong. I knew too much about nutrition and, consequently, was ridden with guilt. I'd lose five or ten pounds, go off the diet or medication, and gain the weight back.

How absurd it all has been. Especially since I am an organic vegetable gardener. I love fresh vegetables and fruit. I also enjoy breads and grains. When I first thought of attempting the Stillman and Atkins diets, I was horrified that fruit was not allowed. I'm fairly active and have, in the past, enjoyed running. My July issue of *Runner's World* came and I read about your diet. The following day I purchased your *Pritikin Permanent Weight-Loss Manual.*

The bookstore was next door to my favorite ice cream parlor. In a totally preplanned move, I walked from that bookstore into the ice cream shop and bought my favorite ice cream cone. I sat in my car reading your book and eating the ice cream. I went home and finished your book that day (it was far more rewarding than the ice cream). The following day I shopped, purchasing lots of fresh produce, Kavli flatbread, matzo meal, dry curd cottage cheese—only items on your shopping list.

I'm learning fast. I've been using the recommended recipes, but not in the order suggested. I made chicken stock the day after I read your book. I've had chicken with mushrooms, fish balls, creamy artichoke dressing, Italian dressing with apple juice, to name a few. I've used the Italian dressing and Dijon mustard to moisten my tuna. It makes a great sandwich on Norwegian flatbread with lots of romaine.

The diet is the best I've ever been on. I'm not retaining water. I don't feel hungry or weak or tired and haven't had any headaches, and I'm not moody or irritable. I expect that I will begin to feel even better as time goes on. For now, I just feel terrific about what I'm doing. I'm relieved that I'm not putting excess strain on my body by consuming fats and

---

*This diet is a low-carbohydrate diet, high in protein and animal fat.

processed foods. I travel regularly and have been away from home three of the eight days. The night before last, in Boston, my scrod and salad with lemon and the one-half baked, plain potato tasted delicious.

I weigh 120 and think 105–110 will be perfect for my 5'3" frame. This time I feel optimistic about making it. You've convinced me of the importance of being the right weight from a health standpoint and provided me with a comfortable way to achieve it.

Voices like yours are really needed in this age of glorification of thin models, vanity, and fad diets. Sound nutritional eating habits, such as you recommend, must be learned. When they are, they become a true gift, a gift of life.

Thank you.

Shelley Tork

We wrote to Shelley a year later. She responded with a phone call to tell us that for 2½ months she stuck to the diet religiously. She said the biggest thing she noticed was the effect on her mental health. She found she was always in a good mood.

When the holidays came, Shelley stopped following the diet as closely. Last February she underwent tests and was put on potent drug therapy because of chest pains. It turned out that the pain was due to a stomach problem. She was told to stay away from coffee, fried foods, and other sources of fats. She went back on the Pritikin diet, and her chest pains disappeared.

The Pritikin diet enables healthy young people in their twenties to become even healthier and to feel better. Some people—like Elena, whose letter is quoted below—feel that they lose control when dining in restaurants. For such people, we sincerely hope that this book will be of assistance.

[Received February 5, 1983]

Dear Dr. Pritikin:

I cannot say that I follow the dietary program to the letter, but I run 3–8 miles a day and the only fat, oil, sugar, and cholesterol I ingest is usually at a restaurant or somewhere out of my control. I was introduced to the program (your book) along with my sister when our father decided to follow it for his heart problem. My sister and I (and, of course, my father) have the utmost respect for you as one of the few respected doctors not taking advantage of this country's obsession with eating and search for an easy way out to reduce their weight. I know my father feels much better, and my sister and I (both in our mid-twenties) both feel and look much healthier. I, for one, plan to follow the program for the rest of my life, and intend to bring up my children in the same way. Although I'm not the preaching type, any chance I have I recommend the Pritikin diet to my friends. I love it, and I've never felt better.

Good luck to you,

Sincerely,
Elena Barere

Elena still follows the diet and intends to do so always. She is 24 years old, and because of her family medical history, she feels fortunate to have been introduced to it so early.

Most people report that shortly after going on the Pritikin diet they feel better. And have a great deal more energy and enthusiasm for life. Here are some comments:

About six weeks ago I saw Mr. Pritikin on the Mike Douglas show and have since been doing my best to restructure my eating habits in line with the Pritikin Program's recommendations. Since that time I have managed to lose 15 pounds as well and feel 15 times better. (Pasadena, Maryland)

After following the diet for one month, I've lost twelve pounds and find that I have an abundance of energy. (Clinton, New Jersey)

We have been on the diet for three months and are true converts. We feel better, have energy to spare, and have no trouble maintaining the weight we want. We've even traveled and visited a lot and, with planning, can avoid having to deviate. We are both in our thirties and see the diet and exercise as part of a permanent part of our lifestyle from now on. We've turned on a lot of others not by talking but by modeling! (Hattiesburg, Missouri)

My husband and I are in our early thirties. Our son is seven. My husband and I spent about fifteen years as practicing alcoholics, and I spent thirty years as a practicing compulsive overeater. Two and a half years ago we joined A.A. [Alcoholics Anonymous] and O.A. [Overeaters Anonymous]. We started to take care of our bodies. Over the two and a half years, we gradually changed our eating habits. When we started the Pritikin Program five months ago, only a few changes had to be made.

We dropped weight immediately. It was the first time in my life that I had to work at gaining weight. . . . I have so much energy there aren't enough hours in a day to get everything done I want to do. (Warrenton, Oregon)

We hope this book will make it easier for you to eat well all the time. We want you to feel as wonderful as the people who wrote these letters.

4

Restaurant Dining, Pritikin Style

*E*ating in restaurants is more than a national pastime—it's become an essential part of the way we choose to live, helping to hold together the fabric of our lives. Virtually everyone is affected to varying degrees, including Pritikin diet followers and would-be followers.

The trend toward frequent restaurant dining is due, in part, to the increased attractiveness of restaurants, both in decor and in quality of food and service. The relaxed ambience shared with a favorite companion, and that delicious meal delivered without our lifting a finger, make the food taste even better and somehow take the sting out of a harried day. It is the healing, renewing quality of a pleasant restaurant experience that has many of us willingly digging deeper into our pockets to pay the bill.

But a more basic reason underlying the popularity of restaurant dining is the influx of women into the job market. More and more couples and families are eating out because the former household "cook"—now a breadwinner too—is just too bushed at the end of the day to put together a meal. A related factor is our peripatetic lifestyle: how many of us are near our kitchens at lunchtime on work days, in particular? Another big chunk of restaurant business consists of meals eaten out while people are on vacation or traveling on business. Come to think of it, the conduct of both business and courtships would probably grind to a halt if business luncheons and dinner dates were for some strange reason to be banned!

The Pritikin Dieter
Dines Out

Given this formidable fact of life, how do you, the Pritikin dieter, fit in? Can you reconcile your desire to follow the Pritikin diet with your practice of eating out once, three times, or a dozen times weekly? Be assured, you needn't become a schizophrenic so far as your eating practices are concerned—good at home but incorrigible once you set foot outside your door. Eating out can be compatible with the Pritikin diet. The growing number of restaurants accommodating Pritikin dieters is, of course, a tremendous help, and this book acquaints you with some of them in many parts of the country. Sometimes you will need to carve your own niche, though. Fortunately, as this book will show, it's possible to go into many restaurants and be served an excellent Pritikin-style meal, when you know how to approach the challenge.

Choosing a Restaurant

In considering where to go on your restaurant outing, you would ideally like to choose Pritikin-oriented restaurants, like those listed in Chapter 8 of this book. That won't always be possible, of course: often, you will be on your own. As a rule, many coffee shops and cafeterias—and certainly fast-food restaurants—are not geared to individualized meals (though you may find notable exceptions); consider them less promising choices. At the other extreme, an ultra-high-style gourmet restaurant may frown upon your wish to alter their masterpieces—you may have to endure feelings of guilt while there. Yet at least their food is custom-prepared and probably could be adapted as you desire, if you're assertive.

Between the extremes there lies a vast middle ground of restaurants that might be suitable for you. Ask to see the menu, if you're not familiar with it, before settling into your seat—to avoid an awkward about-face at the table should it be necessary. Designated health-food or vegetarian restaurants may seem a good pick, but, as will be discussed shortly, they are often misguided in what they consider "healthful." For the most part, don't rely on restaurants to fill your whole-grains quota; at the present time, there are still too few places using whole grains, though the numbers of such restaurants are swelling.

In general, patronize restaurants that are most likely to be able to meet your needs. When in doubt, use the telephone to ascertain in advance whether a restaurant has suitable items or can make minor modifications. Also use the phone to call ahead to restaurants when you wish to make special food requests.

Restaurants in Transition

In response to health-conscious eating trends, many restaurants are emphasizing fresh vegetables and salads and alternatives to red meat such as chicken, fish, and vegetarian dishes. The trend even reverberates to the fast-food chains—witness the advent of the salad bar and the chicken sandwich, in lieu of the ubiquitous hamburger. But many restaurateurs, despite good intentions, do not understand what really constitutes good nutrition; others offer whatever dishes will maximize business. As a result, these more "healthful" menus may feature a dozen egg concoctions, melted-cheese-topped vegetables, high-fat gourmet preparations of chicken or fish, and ingredients such as nuts and honey. Or, because the old idea that vegetable oils are good for you still lingers on, some restaurants brag that they use "healthful" products like pure safflower oil, margarine instead of butter, or nondairy creamers. The fact is that these vegetable-oil foods are just as unhealthful and fattening as the dairy products they replace.

Perusing such menus can be frustrating to Pritikin dieters. But remember that many such restaurants offer whole-grain foods and are at least equipped with fresh vegetables and other suitable raw materials that can be customized to meet your specifications, which gives you a fighting chance. Given some initiative, strength of character, ingenuity, and the practical know-how provided by this book, you should be able to eat out enjoyably without having to check your dietary tenets along with your coat before taking your table.

Attitude Is Key

The most basic tool in the art of restaurant survival is a good attitude. Ideally, we would all like to enter any restaurant in a positive spirit, ready to fend off gustatory temptations and able to handle all circumstances with aplomb. Sounds good, but we may not always be that controlled. There may be moments when we feel wishy-washy about whether to "eat Pritikin" tonight or, more likely, how far to carry it. Or perhaps we're out with friends who, not sharing our dietary convictions, may chide us and eventually lead to our downfall if we're feeling weak-willed. All but the diehard puritans among us will have such occasional lapses. By the way, don't be too hard on yourself if this happens—that can only lead to the refrain "Oh well, what's the use. . . ." Basically, what's needed is a realistic, self-forgiving attitude, combined with a certain self-assurance and an assertive rather than defensive approach. Enter a restaurant believing you deserve to be served what you need and want. Things may not go perfectly, but you will do your best and do it graciously. Congratulate yourself when things go well, and don't berate yourself if you deviate a little from your plan. There's always next time. Besides, as your skills in the art of restaurant survival grow, you should be able to score higher in subsequent restaurant outings. It takes a bit of practice and experience!

A Straightforward Order

If your attitude is one of confidence and resolve, you can be sure it will permeate your restaurant experience. In particular, it will affect that crucial communication with waiter or waitress: your order. You will come across as someone to be taken seriously—and they will notice. Cultivate your ordering skills—even the right attitude won't save you if you garble your instructions or don't speak up. For best results, observe this rule: leave *no ambiguity* when stating your order. Don't assume they can extrapolate, for example, that you want no butter on your vegetables if you've asked for your potato dry. Repeat the order twice, if there is any doubt in your mind that it didn't take 100% the first time, or ask to have the order repeated to you. You can also let them know that if the food isn't prepared right, you'll send it back—this usually ensures that your request won't be taken too casually. Lastly, maintain a sense of humor, be friendly and undemanding yet firm in your tone of voice, and roll with the punches.

Chances are, if you've communicated well, your food will arrive as ordered. If not, you'll be in a better position psychologically to send it back if necessary, knowing you were very clear when you originally ordered it—and the waiter or waitress should readily acknowledge that. Sometimes a problem occurs in the communication step between waiter and chef, when the waiter may overlook the special requests in his haste to get the order out. To avoid that, your waiter must make sure to get the message across to the chef—on paper, orally, or both. You can help by gently reminding him to be certain the kitchen understands before a mishap occurs.

Menu Literacy

Along with the right attitude and good communication techniques, you'll need some proficiency in a skill we've dubbed "menu literacy." This isn't the usual kind of literacy—though the menu could be in a foreign language or refer to unfamiliar culinary terms. What we're talking about is a subtler skill, a bit like reading between the lines. You need to know what menu items hold promise for your meal; what probing questions to ask about styles of preparation; what kinds of dishes lend themselves best to minor substitutions and modifications; and so on. No hard-and-fast rules on the subject exist, but we can supply you with some general guidelines.

First, scan the menu to see how it's organized. Observe the divisions or headings indicating the different categories of foods. Simply organized menus may offer just entrées, side orders, beverages, and desserts; but usually you'll find a more comprehensive rundown, which may also include appetizers, soups, salads, and vegetables. Entrée categories may be broken down into subcategories of beef, poultry, fish, or vegetarian specialties. On breakfast or lunch menus, you'll often see sandwiches, fruits and juices, and egg dishes. Don't overlook any of the categories—each of them may be the source of a delicious meal or snack for you. Even the egg dishes, usually to be avoided, might yield you a nice poached egg white on toast. You may find that the complete-meal package offered, which often includes everything from salad to dessert, is too rigid a set-up for you, even though it may appear to be a better bargain. It may be best for you to order *à la carte* from a number of different menu headings, assembling your own selection of dishes to comprise your meal. This approach is also more suitable if you follow the healthful practice of eating smaller meals throughout the day, and are not hungry enough to handle a four-course spread.

Once you have a feel for the menu style, zero in on the specific offerings. These will vary enormously, depending on the quality, range, and elaborateness of the food on the menu, and may be particularly extensive in some ethnic restaurants. (In the next chapter, we'll go into detail about ordering in the most popular kinds of ethnic restaurants.)

As you check for possibilities, remember this: if an item looks promising, even if it isn't described exactly as you'd want it, see if it can be modified to your design. The key is whether the restaurant has everything made up in advance

49

their way—for example, all the vegetables already bathed in butter or soaking in an oily sauce, or fish or chicken pre-breaded and deep-fried, sitting in a warming tray—or whether the restaurant is more geared to custom orders. Frequently, restaurants are hybrids in this respect, and are able to customize at least some of their dishes.

More pointers on menu literacy are offered in Chapter 6, in which a variety of actual menus is analyzed.

Openers

The instant you are seated by the hostess, be prepared to answer the inevitable query from the cocktail waitress, "Do you wish something from the bar?" Or, earlier in the day, the waitress bearing her steaming coffee pot will descend upon you offering to fill your cup. You could, if you like, order something suitable to sip while you study the menu. We'll provide some suggestions later on in the discussion of beverages.

Appetizers, Soups, Side Orders, and Vegetables

These categories are grouped together because of their potential overlap in different restaurants. For instance, a vegetable such as a steamed artichoke may appear in one restaurant under "vegetables," in another under "appetizers," and in still another with "side orders." Similarly, a bouillon or other acceptable soup could appear under "appetizers" as well as "soups."

Steer clear of major pitfalls like deep-fried vegetables, cream soups, garlic-cheese bread, fondues, stuffed baked potatoes, nachos (fried tortilla chips with melted cheese), and so on. But if you see items like sautéed mushrooms, or broccoli with cheese sauce, you might ask whether the mushrooms could be water- or wine-sautéed, or if the broccoli could be steamed unbuttered and served with a lemon wedge instead of the sauce. A skewered vegetable kabob offered as an appetizer could be a delicious *hors d'oeuvre*—with or without a little meat, chicken, or seafood on it—if the oily basting mixture were replaced by other ingredients. The chef could baste the kabob instead with wine, lemon juice, or tomato juice, adding seasonings such as garlic, ginger, onion, or herbs.

If this sounds a bit complicated, don't forget that many other items can be ordered as is, or nearly so. A wonderful meal opener is a dish of cool, crunchy raw vegetable tidbits, the popular relish tray. Go easy on the vinegared peppers or pickles, which are high-salt items, and pass on the olives (unless you can stop at just one—since they are very high in fat).

If a cheese- or sour-cream–type dip is served with the relishes, ask instead for a spicy salsa—that sensational Mexican staple so popular out West; or even a bottled Tabasco will do. Or just enjoy the vegies *au naturel*. If you are having a vegetarian meal otherwise, you could order a small appetizer of chilled lobster, delicious with a wedge of lemon and a little red cocktail sauce. Or split an order of baby shrimp or crab (which are higher-cholesterol foods) with a table partner.

If you prefer a robust soup for starters, look for one in a greaseless clear stock or tomato base, containing primarily vegetables with such additions as barley, rice, or pasta. Since soups are prepared in advance, there is little you can do to redeem a greasy one short of charming the chef into defatting it in the kitchen. In a pinch, you can skim off much of the fat with your spoon.

Bread or crackers are often served with soups, or at other times during the meal. Be sure to stock up on lots of warm unbuttered bread or muffins if they are sourdough or other virtually fat-free varieties. Many restaurants now offer traditional crusty French sourdough—oil-free and divine. Most crackers, other than some rye crackers, usually contain shortening or oil, and lots of salt. Most whole-wheat breads contain fats, which unfortunately could cancel out the benefits of the whole-grain flours with which they are made.

One possible side order that is a delicious and filling addition to almost any meal is a baked potato. Avoid accidentally getting it with "the works" by specifying that it be "plain." Some fresh chopped chives or green onions, if not already attached to sour cream, are a good potato topping. If the menu is short on other acceptable items, why not order *two* baked potatoes?

Salads

A fresh, crisp salad nicely complements almost any meal. Look for tossed greens and raw vegetable assortments. A bit of seafood in a main-course salad is a treat. Avoid those with dressing already mixed in, such as a Caesar, marinated, or cream-style salad. Order the salad plain—that is, undressed—and request lemon wedges or mild vinegar, such as a wine vinegar, on the side. At a salad bar, you may find peppers in vinegar, which also will add a little zip. Some salad bars offer interesting chilled stewed vegetable combinations, such as tomato, onion, and zucchini, which make a good salad topping if they are not oily. At your table, you can improvise a salad dressing using Tabasco sauce and mustard, or tomato juice if you've ordered it, mixed in with the salad vinegar or lemon. Or, do as some do, and carry a little of your favorite salad dressing with you in a small, tightly closed container.

For practically any dish you order, from vegetables to salad, baked potato, bread, or an entrée like broiled fish or chicken—ask about salsa, mentioned in the discussion of appetizers. It adds a wonderful piquant flavor to any of these foods. Though traditionally a Mexican relish, it has caught on in some American establishments. As an alternative, see if the restaurant has another condiment—like Dijon mustard, a hot sauce such as Picante sauce, or a little soy sauce or even horseradish (uncreamed)—to liven up your food. Use these condiments in *small amounts,* however, as they are high-salt items.

Entrées

Breakfast Entrées

Now that we have dealt with more peripheral menu items, let's talk about the entrée offerings at a given meal. On a breakfast or brunch menu, you are likely to find fancy egg dishes and breakfast meats as featured items. You can breeze by them unless, as suggested earlier, you want to request an egg white poached in water and served on dry toast or a muffin—or maybe even some scrambled egg whites without butter or oil, made with nonfat milk. Salsa or Picante sauce would be a tasty condiment for either egg preparation.

You may also find pancakes and waffles prominent on the menu. With pre-made batters, you assume some egg yolk will be present and possibly some oil. Ask to be sure. If there is a little, you'll have to decide whether you can afford some leeway on your diet. You can still control the cooking by asking for minimal oil on the grill and, of course, for no butter or syrup to be served on top. Try to get a side order of sliced fruit, preferably fresh, as a topping—or if you absolutely must, use a dab of syrup on the side.

Your best breakfast bet, whatever obscure corner of the menu you find it in, is a hot cooked cereal. Oatmeal (rolled oats) and Cream of Wheat are the most common restaurant choices. Oatmeal is preferable, and regular rolled oats are much superior to the instant variety. Order your hot cereal with hot or cold nonfat milk, if you like, and sliced fruit, with plain toast or muffins on the side. The usual array of cold cereals is dismally sugarcoated. Try for Shredded Wheat or Grape-Nuts, to be served with nonfat milk (heated if you'd like a hot cereal). If whole or lowfat milk is all that is available, try using a little water or fruit juice, which some people actually prefer.

Speaking of fruit juice, under ordinary circumstances, order a whole orange, half grapefruit, or other fruit of choice, rather than a glass of juice. The whole fruit is much better for you.

Lunch and Dinner Entrées

On a luncheon menu, you may still see egg dishes—such as quiches, omelettes, and frittatas. Bypass these. Other common lunch items are sandwiches, normally made to order except in a cafeteria, and therefore easily customized. Hold the mayonnaise, butter, or dressing on the bread (try mustard). Get a heaping helping of salad vegetables (shredded lettuce and/or sprouts, sliced tomato, cucumber, onion, and perhaps a thin slice of pickle) and a smallish portion of sliced breast of turkey or chicken (optional).

You may have to pass on a tuna-salad sandwich, if the tuna's hopelessly mixed in a mayonnaise base. But if tuna is what you like, you might persuade the kitchen to open a fresh can (only water-packed will do) and sprinkle some lemon juice or wine vinegar on it with a few seasonings like dill, garlic, or onion. However, if you can select a vegetarian sandwich that meets Pritikin guidelines (no avocado, peanut butter, Swiss cheese, etc.), you'll have more leeway for your dinner choices. Pita ("pocket") bread, if they serve it, works admirably well for any of these overstuffed sandwich concoctions. You can even order a green salad and stuff that into a pita shell for a salad-and-sandwich-in-one.

You may have a harder time getting a baked potato at lunch, with the supremacy of the French fry. But try; maybe they'll zap one in a microwave just for you.

Hot lunch (featuring poultry, fish, vegetables, or pasta) and dinner menu items may be the same, often the main difference being just the price. Have you ever noticed a lunch entrée suddenly get more valuable after 5:00 P.M.? This can make you a fan of early-hour dinners! Nonetheless, your main concern with these dishes is the mode of preparation. If the menu doesn't go into enough detail, you may need to ask incisive questions, such as: "Is there butter, oil, or other fat added to the dish, and, if so, how heavily?" A meal of baked sole in wine sauce, for example, could be a good choice. However, you'll want to know what's in the sauce besides the wine, and whether the fish has been sautéed in butter or oil before baking. If the reply spells R-I-C-H, ask whether some sole can be poached in plain wine or lemon juice and water, seasoned with dill or other spices.

If your portion of fish or poultry seems to exceed your daily allotment, consider splitting it with your meal companion, take the surplus home in a doggy bag, or splurge—but eat cholesterol-free meals for the next day or two. Or you may be better off with a casserole-type dish that contains a small amount of meat or fish—but only if the fat content seems minimal. If this is not the case, you may need to pass up such dishes unless the kitchen is in a position to modify the preparation for you.

As for accompaniments on the entrée plate, stay with the baked potato rather than the usually oily rice pilaf. If a vegetable is served, ask whether it is unbuttered; or else see whether a vegetable might be custom-steamed for you.

Beverages and Desserts

If you like a beverage with your meal, keep your water glass filled with ice water. Or ask the cocktail waitress for a Perrier or other good mineral water, or a low-salt club soda (try the new Canada Dry variety), over ice with a slice of lemon or lime. You could have this served to you with V-8 or tomato juice, half and half. For a hot beverage, a pot of hot water with lemon is satisfying, or brew it weakly with a little decaffeinated coffee if you're having coffee withdrawals. Whenever it is available, opt for herb tea. Or bring your own herb tea bag.

Desserts, those naughty enticements, can be hard to ignore. Just stand firm and ask what fresh fruit is available. Melon, berries, grapefruit, or a mixed fruit cup are all nice meal endings. If you know of a restaurant offering special low-calorie dessert creations, you could inquire as to the fat or sugar content; then weigh your decision wisely. If you can't restrain yourself, the best choice would be a fruit ice or sorbet (containing sugar but no fat or eggs), which brings us to the subject of indiscretions in general.

Indiscretions

Try as you may, there will probably be times in restaurants when you do compromise your dietary principles. Indiscretions sometimes stem from situations beyond our control, like the chef's imperfect rendering of your special request, which you may decide is not serious enough to warrant a complaint. As an example, you might notice your broiled fish glistening suspiciously, though you had asked for it to be broiled without butter or oil. The waiter assures you that your instructions were followed, confirming it with the chef, and suggests that the fish may have absorbed a little oil from the cooking surface. Rather than make a scene, since they apparently tried to follow your directions, you decide to leave well enough alone. In such cases, it can be worth a small deviation in exchange for maintaining a working rapport with the restaurant. Besides, you're hungry! On the other hand, don't sheepishly accept food if a major blunder has been made in your order. Then, if the waiter tries to talk you into accepting it or is reluctant to take it back, by all means express your displeasure.

Indiscretions can also be deliberate on your part. Realistically, even the best of us may recall occasions when we have chosen to stretch our diet limits—perhaps a bit too far—while resolving to make up for the lapse in the coming week. Should you find yourself overcome by the impulse to "cheat," at least do it sensibly! Review the list of various dietary substances to avoid in excess (page 5), beginning with the worst—cholesterol—and proceeding in descending order to those less deleterious.

Indiscretions, however, can often be too great a risk for anyone with a health problem such as diabetes, elevated blood pressure, or any other diagnosed cardiac abnormality. Moreover, we advise everyone to keep tabs on his or her blood cholesterol and triglycerides levels with an annual blood test. Cholesterol levels should not exceed 100 plus your age, or a maximum of 160 mg/dl.* Triglycerides should not exceed 125 mg/dl.

Special Arrangements with Restaurants

Say you're on a vacation and will be eating frequent meals in your hotel. Perhaps you are a luncheon regular at a local café near work, or you may have a favorite dinner spot you gravitate to on weekends. In these or other cases where your repeat business is substantial, you would gain by having a more formal understanding with the restaurant management. Explain your dietary needs to the restaurateur and/or chef in some detail. Their degree of accommodation to you will depend on their facilities, their flexibility, and, of course, their desire to please. Do your utmost to enlist their cooperation.

---

*mg/dl = milligrams per deciliter (a ratio of substance weight to blood volume).

Offer to call before coming in to allow them more notice. Even supply them with information on special foods you may want that they don't normally stock, such as nonfat milk, brown rice, fat-free whole-grain bread or breakfast cereal, or fresh fruit. You might share favorite recipes with a willing chef, who could add them to his repertoire as "special meals" and might even list them on the menu, as many restaurants have done. A more adventuresome chef might wish to create· his own gastronomical delights in this new culinary form.

Many restaurants will be very supportive. They value their patrons' satisfaction and will rise graciously to the challenge you present. Don't, however, necessarily expect enthusiastic support during your first visit to all restaurants. Sometimes your needs may be viewed as too great an infringement or inconvenience. But don't give up and stop voicing your requirements. It will take some education and a lot of consumer demand for many more restaurants to begin to serve healthful fare.

Additional Advice

A few miscellaneous hints are well worth noting. You can always bring along some of your own rations in a "restaurant survival kit" tucked into your purse or pocket. These might include one or more items such as: salad dressing, salsa or other topping or dip, bread, bran, rice, fruit, or herb tea bag. If you are celebrating a birthday or other occasion, you might even bring your own cake or pie, but be sure to advise the restaurant in advance. Any carry-in items should be placed in small, spillproof containers. A restaurant survival kit is especially useful when your choices are going to be fairly limited and you want to add a little flair to your meal. It's best to be discreet about this, needless to say.

Another technique, though not as much fun, is to snack at home beforehand—enough to take the edge off your appetite so that you won't feel starved or overindulge wildly in the restaurant. This tactic is sometimes necessary when you don't know the restaurant or when you do know that the restaurant has an inflexible, very un-Pritikin menu and will not cater to special requests.

Once you are seated in a restaurant, remember these suggestions:

- *Study the menu with an open mind.* Be creative; experiment with ordering from different parts of the menu to assemble your meal, and note possible minor modifications that would make a dish acceptable.

- *Communicate effectively.* Give your waiter your instructions for the order clearly and assertively, but pleasantly. Express appreciation when merited.

A final piece of advice: never underestimate the effect that your requests can have on a restaurant's future cuisine. Most restaurant eaters make few comments, either positive or negative, on the nature of the foods being offered; you will be remembered if you do. Keep asking for what you want, whether it be whole grains, fresh fruit, or oil-free sauces. Let's create a demand for healthful restaurant food!

5

Ethnic Cuisines

Nowadays it is fairly common for people to dine at an ethnic restaurant, particularly for dinner. Since ethnic restaurants, with their individual styles of cooking, offer special challenges to the Pritikin dieter, we are treating this subject separately in this chapter. Happily, Chinese, Italian, and Mexican cuisine lend themselves rather well to Pritikin requirements. So people who love these foods, if they are armed with a few basic pointers as provided herein, can usually order quite satisfactory meals without too much difficulty.

Some of the other ethnic cuisines may be less promising for people who seek to keep their complex-carbohydrate intake up and their fat and cholesterol intakes down. But if for some reason you are confronted with the problem of ordering "Pritikin" in one of these less favorable situations, it's well to know what the special pitfalls are so that you will be able to order the best possible meal with minimal hassle and compromise of your dietary guidelines.

For example, you wouldn't ordinarily seek out a restaurant serving French *haute cuisine* as a good place to find a Pritikin meal. Yet, even in this unlikely milieu, it is often possible to secure a satisfactory meal, as the experiences of Barbara Harris and her husband have shown. The Harrises, both Pritikin diet devotées, toured France for a month, and reported their culinary successes in a *New York Times* article. They dined at inns, restaurants, and hotels, as well as picnicking. (See pages 75–80.)

In this chapter, we'll tour restaurants serving the most popular ethnic cuisines—Chinese, Italian, and Mexican—and other restaurants serving Japanese, Indian, and Jewish food, as well as the forbidding French cuisine. Some general principles emerge that should be helpful in any kind of ethnic restaurant.

Dining in a
Chinese Restaurant

Chinese cookery has won acclaim as perhaps the world's most exquisite cuisine. Fortunately for Pritikin diners, one of the most popular techniques used in the preparation of Chinese food—stir-frying—can be adapted admirably to our requirements. Stir-fried Chinese dishes abound with fresh, crisp, lightly cooked vegetables generally combined with smaller amounts of poultry, meat, or seafood. Since in most Chinese restaurants each order is cooked separately, it is usually possible to have the dishes customized to your specifications. Served with rice, a stir-fried Chinese dish can be a small banquet.

Some Chinese vegetables have become quite familiar in the United States—water chestnuts, snow peas, bamboo shoots, Chinese cabbage; other vegetables, like daikon and oriental mushrooms, are less familiar. Some of the vegetables used, like bell peppers and tomatoes, are staples in many cuisines.

Chinese cuisine makes liberal use of onions and garlic, and foods are variously seasoned with fresh ginger, soy sauce, dry sherry, vinegar, Chinese hot mustard, and other condiments. Chicken broth or water usually forms the base for sauces, which are frequently thickened with cornstarch. Cantonese dishes are generally milder, and Hunan and Szechuan dishes are usually spicy hot. Some restaurants feature hot curries, a seasoning borrowed from Indian cuisine in fairly recent history.

Stir-frying is done in a large pan with high, sloped sides called a wok. Characteristically, lard, peanut oil, or other oils are used as the medium for cooking. Studies have shown that peanut oil is particularly conducive to the development of arterial blockage, but any oil or fat should be shunned by Pritikin dieters. When you order your stir-fried dish in a Chinese restaurant, ask to have the dish cooked in chicken broth (which has usually been skimmed of its fat) or in water instead of oil or lard. If this instruction appears to pose difficulties, ask that only the barest minimum of oil or lard be used in the wok, since a very small amount is quite adequate to cook the foods.

The steamed white rice accompanying your entrée is a reasonable option for restaurant dining if you are eating plenty of whole grain otherwise, and it is much preferred to fried rice. (Fried rice may *look* like brown rice, but it isn't. It owes its color in Chinese cooking to soy sauce.)

Dairy products are rarely used in Chinese cooking, but

bean curd (tofu), a custardlike ingredient made from soybeans, appears in many dishes. Fresh bean curd can be boiled, simmered, stir-fried, shallow-fried, or deep-fried. (Its pressed version, from which water has been extracted, can also be cooked in various ways.) The bean curd is then cut into small chunks and added to stir-fried and other dishes. Although bean curd contains no cholesterol, it is as high as or higher in fat than many animal products and is very high in protein, so it should be regarded as a substitute for poultry, fish, or meat and considered part of your daily protein allotment. Choose steamed or simmered tofu, of course, rather than fried tofu.

In addition to stir-fried items, other dishes suitable for Pritikin diners may be prepared by steaming or roasting. You'll need to make inquiries in each restaurant. When you place your order, be sure to tell the waiter that in addition to wanting to avoid oil or lard, you wish no MSG (monosodium glutamate, a sodium compound), sugar, or salt to be used. If you wish, have them use just a little soy sauce in cooking your order; or have them omit that, too. Then, when you receive your food, you can add a little soy sauce or some Chinese hot mustard (which will already be on your table, or your waiter can bring them) to suit your tastes.

Generally, if you state your requirements and are in a Chinese restaurant that prepares dishes fresh, as most do, you'll have a wide selection to choose from. Many Chinese restaurants have a vegetarian plate called Buddha's Delight (request it steamed) and a vegetable-and-chicken plate called moo goo gai pan. Both dishes are very adaptable to Pritikin diet guidelines. If these are not available, you might ask for plain steamed vegetables, perhaps with a little added chicken. Sometimes Chinese restaurants leave a little skin on chicken; it's a good idea to ask to have it removed before cooking. Don't order any of the mo-shu dishes. Mo-shu, in Chinese, means yellow cassia blossoms, and in dishes by that name they are symbolized by tiny pieces of scrambled egg, sometimes almost indistinguishable among the other ingredients.

Keep in mind that Chinese tea contains stimulants just as regular tea does. You might ask for a pot of hot water to use to dilute the tea. A little tea flavors the plain water quite adequately.

Several of the Chinese restaurants listed in Chapter 8 of this book can offer 40 or more selections Pritikin-style. It would almost be worth a trip from other parts of the country just to partake!

Additional information on Chinese restaurants appears on pages 104–108.

Dining in an
Italian Restaurant

Italian cuisine, that inspired segment of gastronomy, ranks high on almost everyone's list of preferred food styles, and good Italian restaurants are common in American cities everywhere. Italian food and pasta are practically synonymous, a most fortunate circumstance for Pritikin diners. A plate of pasta with a suitable sauce, a salad, and bread make a wonderful luncheon or dinner just by themselves—high in complex carbohydrates and low in fat and cholesterol.

Pasta dough, made from wheat flour and water, is rolled out and cut into different sizes and shapes, each with its own distinctive name, and is cooked in either dried or fresh form. Whole eggs or egg yolks are sometimes worked into pasta dough; such pastas should, of course, be avoided. Unless you are eating pasta in a natural foods restaurant, it will very likely be made from refined wheat rather than from whole-grain flour, so you won't get the fiber and nutrients present in the whole grain. But if you are eating plenty of whole grains at other times, this is an acceptable compromise for restaurant dining. The somewhat dense and chewy basic Italian bread is made simply of flour, water, and salt, so it has a nutritional composition equivalent to that of most pasta.

Choose a tomato sauce to accompany your pasta that is meat-free, as in a basic marinara sauce, or have a little of the meat sauce. Request that the sauce served you have no olive oil in it, if possible. You'll find most marinara sauces—seasoned as they are with garlic, basil, oregano, bay leaves, parsley, and wine—quite delicious over hot pasta.

Pasta of suitable shapes is often used to create entrées stuffed with meat and cheese, as in manicotti, tortellini, and cannelloni. All can easily be made Pritikin-style, with the right ingredients, but they are rarely served that way in a restaurant. If you are able to make cooking recommendations, and if the demand is there, the chef might just create a new menu item for a Pritikin-style stuffed pasta entrée.

Fish and shellfish complement many Italian dishes, as do poultry and a variety of meats. Chickpeas and fava beans are used frequently in basic Italian cooking and occasionally appear on Italian-American restaurant menus. When you order your meal, control the portion of lean meat, seafood, or poultry and help yourself to oil-free beans, if available. Avoid all cheeses (which will not be skim-milk cheeses), and request that your pasta not come to you already sprinkled with Parmesan cheese.

In some Italian restaurants, pizza can be customized to meet Pritikin guidelines. The basic dough is comparable to pasta dough. Ask whether the cheese can be omitted and the pizza topped with the restaurant's basic tomato sauce and vegetables, such as sliced tomatoes, mushrooms, bell peppers, onions, and even a few chopped pepperoncinis (peppers in wine vinegar). The potato gnocchi on some restaurant menus may also be suitable. Ask whether they have been made without oil and eggs; some gnocchi recipes simply call for flour and boiled potatoes. Gnocchi, topped with a tomato sauce, is a heavenly dish.

Soups in some Italian restaurants can be quite acceptable. Check out the restaurant's minestrone soup or other vegetable-bean soups. A basic dinner salad can lighten up an Italian meal. Order it without cheese or olives, and use wine vinegar or lemon juice as a dressing. Most Italian restaurants will steam some fresh vegetables (remember to say "hold the butter"). Try a steamed artichoke or some zucchini. And for dessert, stay with fresh fruit when it is available.

See pages 109–114 for a further discussion of Italian restaurants.

Dining in a Mexican Restaurant

Restaurants serving Mexican food are beginning to catch the fancy of Pritikin diners, especially in the West and Southwest. It's easy to understand why: Mexican cuisine is distinctive and delicious and can also be very nutritious, featuring as it does such carbohydrate staples as corn, red beans, rice, and various fresh vegetables, especially chilis and other peppers and tomatoes.

Mexican cooking is characterized by tortillas and chili peppers. Chilis of all sizes, shapes, flavors, colors, and degrees of hotness are used. While only a few people (with "asbestos mouths") relish the hottest chilis, all palates can enjoy the milder ones, which impart a wonderful zestiness to most Mexican dishes without being too potent.

Tortillas are the counterparts of the bread of northern countries. These thin, pancakelike rounds are made of either corn flour, lime, and water (corn tortillas) or wheat flour, water, and lard (flour tortillas). Of course, choose corn tortillas (which are made without lard) when you select food in a Mexican restaurant. Many restaurants offer their patrons a bowl of fried corn tortilla chips along with some hot salsa as a complimentary appetizer. Fried tortillas are "no-no's," but you can ask for a basket or plate of steamed corn tortillas instead. And in some restaurants, there may be a complimentary serving of a mixture of chilis (hot!) with bits of carrots and other ingredients which is usually oil-free or nearly so.

When used to wrap meat, poultry, seafood, beans, or cheese—and then sometimes covered with sauces—tortilla dishes are called enchiladas, burritos, tacos, flautas, or chimichangas. If these items are baked rather than fried and made with corn tortillas, they may be acceptable entrées, but omit any cheese toppings and avoid cheese fillings.

Most salsas are made with chilis, tomatoes, onions, and cilantro (Mexican or Chinese parsley) and, in most restaurants, do not contain oil. Salsas are wonderful toppings for plain warmed corn tortillas, rice, beans, green salads, and other foods. (In conventional American restaurants, particularly steak houses, you may be able to combine a baked potato with a salsa topping for a real taste treat!)

Frijoles, which are hardy pinto or red beans, are a fine choice when they are cooked in a clear broth. Cooked in this manner, they are called frijoles de olla. Unfortunately, most Mexican restaurants in the United States prefer to serve the refried variety—frijoles refritos—made by frying the cooked beans in lard or oil. If you are planning to dine in a Mexican restaurant, try calling ahead in the morning to ask to have the chef save you some plain beans cooked in broth. Most restaurants will gladly do this if they don't buy their refried beans ready-made.

Chicken enchiladas can be an excellent choice. They are generally made with corn tortillas (not fried), filled with deliciously seasoned chicken, and basted or baked in a mild tomato sauce (often oil-free) or covered with salsa de tomatillo, a sauce made with small, sweet green tomatoes. Remember to ask to have the cheese, sour cream, and guacamole (avocado dip) omitted; your heart will thank you. Replace those high-fat toppings with a heaping garnish of finely shredded lettuce, diced tomato, green onion, even thinly sliced cucumber, piled on tostada-style. (Get a big plate of these raw vegetables as a side dish and pile them on the enchiladas yourself.) Or simply ask for a salad and use the vegetables in the same way over the enchiladas (though the finely shredded and chopped vegetables are nicer for this purpose).

Many Mexican restaurants also specialize in fish dishes, a delicious and popular one being red snapper or white fish served with a tasty vegetable tomato sauce—à la Veracruzana.

If the prepared entrées are not suitable, why not create your own dish? Make a Pritikin tostada by spreading some of your side order of beans, as is or mashed, over a corn tortilla that has been oven-heated to crispness. Top with raw vegetables, as described for the chicken enchilada; with salsa or a hot sauce; and with a little shredded chicken, also ordered on the side. Or roll these ingredients in a soft steamed corn tortilla. The kitchen may even be willing to prepare your customized tostada or taco for you.

You may wish to have Mexican rice with your meal. This is usually cooked in a light tomato sauce with a bit of onion. Although the rice is often prepared without oil, you should check this with the cook in order to be sure.

The traditional Mexican dessert—a rich egg custard called flan—is not one to indulge in. Always ask for fresh fruit. If nothing else, the restaurant may have whole oranges, which are often used, sliced, as a garnish.

Dining in a
Japanese Restaurant

Sushi bars and Japanese restaurants are among the newer ethnic food crazes in many American cities. Dare Pritikin-dieters enter?

The range of selections suitable for you will be limited, in part because of the unusually high salt content of Japanese foods. Japan has a high incidence of hypertension and stroke. In northeastern Japan, the rates are the highest in the world, and young and old alike are afflicted. Medical research implicates the Japanese diet because it is so high in salt, made so by foods such as shoyu (soy sauce), miso (fermented soybean paste), pickled vegetables, and salted fish. Among those groups of Japanese whose intake of salt is *not* high, the incidence of hypertension and stroke is correspondingly low.

On the other hand, the low-fat and low-cholesterol intake of the Japanese—rice and noodles are the mainstays of their diet—gives them one of the lowest heart-disease death rates in the world.

You may have other health concerns when you are considering dining in a Japanese restaurant. You may be bothered by the possibility that there will be parasites in the raw fish served at sushi bars. In actuality, the problem seems to be limited to raw salmon, which may occasionally be infested with tapeworms. In Japan, the problem is controlled by the government recommendation to freeze the salmon (thus killing the parasite) before preparing it to be served. In the United States, salmon for use in creations from the sushi bar is frozen, salted, or smoked (like lox)—but if the temperature of smoking is not high enough, the parasites can survive. If you are concerned about this possibility, ask the restaurateur about the restaurant's method of handling salmon or avoid the salmon preparations.

Another health matter when dining in a Japanese restaurant involves the possible presence of talc on the rice. Talc may harbor asbestos fibers, a known carcinogen, and epidemiological studies have shown that the Japanese have a lower incidence than Americans of almost every kind of cancer, with the exception of stomach cancer. While talc-coated rice is now prohibited in Japan, it is available in the United States where it may be purchased in Oriental food stores. Japanese-Americans who traditionally prefer this type of rice may use it in their commercial establishments. You can check this out with the particular restaurant owner.

Health concerns—potential or actual—aside, Japanese food holds great appeal for many Westerners. Part of the appeal is aesthetic—the art of food presentation reaches heights not found elsewhere. At the sushi bar, the customer sits transfixed as the sushi chef deftly prepares sushi (cold vinegar-dressed rice coordinated with fish and other ingredients) or sashimi (thin slices of fish without rice). At your table, a kimono-clad waitress may preside with graceful flourish over a cooking vessel, preparing before your eyes a one-pot dish or nabemono. The adventurous palate is delighted by the exotic nature of Japanese fare: creations from the sushi bar made with raw fish, parboiled octopus, and seaweed—or one-pot dishes with strange-looking ingredients such as the thin transparent gelatinous noodles that float in sukiyaki broth.

Pritikin dieters might like a one-pot dish called mizutaki. As traditionally made, the dish contains cabbage, carrots, watercress, Japanese mushrooms, tofu, and small pieces of chicken. Ask to have the chicken skinned before cooking, if possible, or remove the skin yourself. Sukiyaki, another one-pot dish made with thin slices of a steak-quality beef, might exceed your daily fat and cholesterol allotments, especially if the beef serving is generous. Consider some of the fish dishes, such as halibut simmered in broth. Ask to have salt, soy sauce, sugar, and MSG omitted from any dish you order, if possible, and use a little of the condiments on your table to add extra flavor to your food. Of course, you'll have to pass up the fried foods, including batter-fried tempura dishes.

Soups and raw vegetable salads or relishes are an integral part of a Japanese meal. Soup is even eaten at breakfast. At a Japanese restaurant, you are likely to be served a soup made with a clear broth from a stock (dashi) whose chief components are two dried ingredients—a form of kelp (seaweed) and bonito flakes. Various ingredients will be floating in the soup, such as small bits of fish, chicken, or tofu, and a vegetable such as Japanese onions or some seaweed. Salads are usually tossed with a dressing that is made with vinegar, sugar, salt, soy sauce, and MSG. Relishes are often salt-pickled. The rice used in making sushi is also mixed with vinegar that has been flavored with salt and sugar. It will be difficult to avoid soy sauce, salt, MSG, and sugar in soups, salads, and sushi.

However careful you attempt to be, your meal in a Japanese restaurant will probably be higher in salt than your usual meals, so if you do eat Japanese food, do so only infrequently. Or, at your favorite Japanese restaurants, cultivate the chefs and charm them into preparing you some special dishes, Pritikin-style!

Dining in a French Restaurant

French *haute cuisine,* a gastronomic road paved with béchamel sauce, appeals to many food sophisticates in pursuit of what they consider the ultimate eating experience. Never mind that French sauces are laden with butter, cream, eggs, and cheese—such determined gourmet diners are living for the moment. French culinary masterpieces do have a way of creating desire, but the pleasure they provide is short-lived.

What should you do if you find yourself in a French restaurant in the company of such food enthusiasts? With luck your chef will be an adherent of the newer dictates of *cuisine minceur* (literally, cuisine of slimness), developed by Michel Guérard. In an effort to reform French cooking, he eliminated some of the traditional cooking techniques that caused the diner to grow more rotund with every meal.

Look for the dishes that are prepared by poaching, steaming, or roasting. Poached fish, prepared in a flavorful fat-free liquid stock, and roast chicken are attractive choices. Asparagus in season is a dish some people swoon over. Order asparagus steamed, with a wedge of lemon, or ask for a steamed artichoke, served hot or chilled, or mushrooms, similarly prepared. Hopefully, you may find other acceptable choices among the vegetables, such as stewed leeks, onions simmered in wine vinegar, and diced fresh tomatoes. Inquire about whether they can be prepared without olive oil or butter.

Don't be afraid to ask your waiter what all those French words mean on the menu. After all, it's your stomach and your heart, and only you know what they can handle. If you are finding it difficult to make a selection from the menu, discuss your preferences for style of preparation with the waiter. Pritikin diners know that a haughty waiter can be easily won over with a friendly smile.

Many classic French dishes, such as quiche and crêpe, are taboo because of the egg yolks or other high-cholesterol/high-fat ingredients. But you can order ratatouille niçoise (baked zucchini, eggplant, and tomatoes). This vegetable casserole, which originated in Provence, will have a little oil in it but is otherwise acceptable.

And if you are overcome by a desire to taste a classic French sauce, order it on the side, take a tiny taste, and then leave the rest. You'll be infinitely happier with yourself the next day if you do.

Conclude your meal with an order of fresh fruit or, if available, fruits that have been poached in wine. Pears or other seasonal fresh fruits in red wine, well prepared, are a French delight for which we should all be grateful.

Dining in an
Indian Restaurant

Indian cooking varies greatly according to regional style. Much of North India follows the Islamic Mughlai (Moghul) tradition of food preparation, which has been greatly influenced by Persian culture. Extensive use of meat, rice pilafs, highly fragrant spices and saffron, and dairy ingredients such as milk and yogurt are characteristic of this cuisine. In other areas of India, the style of cooking is often entirely vegetarian and the food is much lighter. Most Indian restaurants in America reflect the North Indian influence.

Until recently, clarified butter or usli ghee (ghee means fat; usli means pure) was used exclusively as a cooking medium. But because butter is too expensive for most Indians, less costly vegetable shortenings and vegetable oils have replaced it in most cases. Usli ghee, however, is believed to possess special attributes and is favored for certain dishes, as well as for some nonculinary purposes. Hindu children are often given a spoonful of usli ghee daily as brain food (in the way American children used to be given cod-liver oil); and hot fomentations of usli ghee and turmeric are sometimes used for healing.

The lavish use of fat in most Indian foods makes it difficult to get a Pritikin-OK meal in Indian restaurants, and the following discussion suggests the best choices from a not-too-auspicious collection.

Fortunately, bread (called roti) is the staff of life in North Indian homes where chapatis, unleavened bread made of whole-wheat flour and water, are prepared daily. Chapatis and other kinds of unleavened griddle-baked breads are suitable and delicious. Avoid fried unleavened breads, especially the deep-fried breads such as poori. Leavened bread generally contains oil and other ingredients to be avoided, so you probably should pass on a leavened bread known as naan, frequently served in Indian restaurants.

Besides their roti, Indians eat prodigious amounts of rice. Rice dishes usually have lots of ghee or other fats incorporated into them, but you might try asking for plain steamed rice. If ghee hasn't been added to the rice in the cooking process, your waiter may be able to serve you some plain rice. The more elaborate rice dishes, such as the pilafs and biryanis (meat or fish and rice casseroles), will be even more oiled. As in Chinese restaurants, don't expect to find brown rice in an Indian restaurant.

Legume dishes, called dals, are another Indian staple. Sometimes they are pureed and used for dipping bread or spooning over rice. They are made with lots of salt, and clarified butter or oil is often mixed into the legumes after they are pureed. If you can rescue dal from the kitchen before the ghee is added, you may have a dish to consider.

Even the best choices in an Indian restaurant require some compromise. For instance, Tandoori chicken, so named because it is traditionally cooked in a tandoor, or Indian clay oven, will have some—though usually not much—added fat. This barbecued chicken dish is prepared by marinating the raw, skinned chicken in a mixture of yogurt and spices, and then brushing it with ghee before placing it on a skewer and setting it into the oven for roasting. (If broiled in a conventional oven, it will probably be basted during the cooking process as well.) When you order this dish, you'll be getting a little fat from the yogurt marinade (the yogurt is probably made from whole milk) as well as from the ghee used for basting. Selecting the chicken breast, rather than the thigh or leg, and eating only a small portion would reduce your fat as well as cholesterol intake considerably.

The Indian restaurant in which you are dining may also offer other dishes prepared in the style of Tandoori cooking. Look for skewered chunks of chicken, known as Tikka Kabobs, or skewered fish. In many parts of India, whole fish, often some kind of white fish, are prepared in this manner. An unusual feature of Tandoori cooking is the addition of a bright orange vegetable dye to the marinade, which gives the food its characteristic color.

The best vegetarian choices in an Indian restaurant will also be a compromise, but since you'll be avoiding the fat and cholesterol of chicken or other animal foods, you'll probably come out even or better. If you are curious about sampling several Indian dishes, consider a vegetarian thali—a thali is a large metal plate containing several small bowls, which hold about half a cup each. You could ask for plain rice, a pureed dal, a yogurt-based dish such as chickpeas and yogurt, and one or two vegetable dishes. Accompanied by a suitable bread such as chapatis, your meal would be quite ample, though you won't have escaped ingesting some ghee.

Indian vegetable dishes are generally classified as "dry" or "wet," depending on whether or not there is a sauce. The dry vegetable dishes usually have less ghee, and some vegetables, such as cauliflower, tend to absorb less ghee from the cooking surface than others. (Eggplant seems to soak it up like a sponge.) In an Indian restaurant, a waiter customarily serves you your food from a serving bowl. So if you order a wet Indian dish such as curry, vegetarian or otherwise, you can minimize the amount of ghee transferred to your plate by asking the waiter to drain off as much of the sauce as possible before serving the food to you.

Raw vegetable salads, such as we know them, do not appear in Indian cuisine, but you'll find dishes such as raitas (yogurt mixed with raw vegetables or fruits), pickled vegetables, and chutneys, served as relishes. Chutneys may be sweet, sour, or sweet-and-sour; spicy or mild; hot or cold. Sometimes oil or clarified butter is used, but more often an excessive amount of salt and sugar will be the offending ingredients.

In India, fresh fruits are traditionally offered at the end of a meal, but in an Indian restaurant, you are more likely to be offered a rich and very sweet dessert. Indian desserts are often made with an unusual form of concentrated whole milk, as well as ghee. They're interesting but hardly suitable Pritikin fare, which is a fair comment about Indian restaurant food in general, thanks to the ubiquitous ghee.

P.S.: Indian gourmets frequently have phenomenally high cholesterol levels—in the 400's!

Dining in a Jewish Restaurant

At the mention of a Jewish deli or restaurant, visions of pastrami sandwiches, sour pickles, chicken soup with matzo balls, knishes, blintzes, and chopped liver dance before one's eyes. The Jewish word for foods that are not kosher is "treyf."

We have to ask whether, from a health standpoint, *most* of the traditional Jewish dishes should be considered treyf—at least for Pritikin diners. Chopped liver is a no-no however it is made, since liver and other organ meats are exceptionally high in cholesterol. Many other foods commonly found on menus in Jewish delis and restaurants are taboo as made—although it is possible to make some of these dishes within the Pritikin guidelines in your own kitchen. So it may seem that attempting to dine in such places is an exercise in futility. But this is not necessarily so.

If you pop in for lunch, you will usually find some soups on the menu, one of which will probably be a vegetable-type variety. This will contain more salt than you've been having, but it will probably be all right from other standpoints. Breast of turkey or chicken and lean roast beef will probably be available for sandwiches. Ask to have just a little sliced poultry or meat, lots of lettuce and sliced tomato, and rye or sour-dough bread (or a water bagel), spread with a little mustard, if desired. The standard pickle accompaniment will be very high in salt, because it has been pickling in the brine for weeks, and the cole slaw often offered will have a mayonnaise dressing. Most delis make their own cole slaw, potato salad, and the like, so it might be possible for your waiter or waitress to provide you with plain shredded cabbage and a little vinegar or lemon. It's worth asking.

If you know in advance that you will be having dinner at the restaurant, you might arrange beforehand for some minor modifications, if the chef is amenable. For instance, if it's chicken soup you crave, ask to have the soup chilled and the fat removed before the soup is reheated and served to you. Substitute plain matzo or matzo farfel (matzo broken into little bits) for the matzo balls. Most Jewish restaurants offer a variety of fish and chicken dishes, as well as specialties such as stuffed cabbage. The cabbage is generally filled with rice mixed with a little beef and spices (or it may be prepared as a vegetarian dish with raisins and/or nuts). With advance notification, perhaps the chef can make minor modifications in a dish for you, such as omitting the nuts (if used) from the stuffed cabbage. If it's fish you want, order it broiled without fat or oil and basted with a little lemon juice; or ask to have it poached in a fat-free broth. Broiled or roasted chicken, without skin and not basted with fats, is another option. Boiled or baked potatoes and butter-free vegetables can round out your meal, together with a tossed green salad with a sprinkling of vinegar or a wedge of lemon, and lots of rye bread.

Extensive use of chicken or beef fat and whole eggs makes many traditional Jewish dishes unacceptable. So, from the

Pritikin dieter's perspective you need to pass up kishke, knishes, kreplach, and knaidlach as "katastrophic." But kasha, or buckwheat groats, could be quite acceptable. Used as a grain in central Europe and other areas, this flavorful, nutritious food is generally prepared by mixing the groats with an unbeaten egg and roasting the coated groats in a skillet until browned. Boiling water is then added (sometimes along with a little chicken fat), and the groats are covered and cooked until tender. A friendly chef could be prevailed upon to prepare groats for you using only the white of an egg and omitting the optional chicken fat. Kasha is sometimes also cooked with mushrooms or mixed after cooking with bow noodles (kasha varnishkas). Either version could be acceptable, but make sure the noodles are not the egg-yolk type.

When it's dessert time, pass up the strudel and cheese cake (which contain oil, butter, eggs, cream cheese, and so forth in abundance), and opt for fresh fruit.

Language Cards
for Foreign Travel

Planning some foreign travel? You might copy these and tuck them in your wallet to use in emergency situations!

HOW TO ORDER YOUR PRITIKIN-SPANISH MEAL
(show this to your waiter)

SIN ACEITE, SIN SAL, Y SIN AZÚCAR.
ESPECIALMENTE SIN "MSG." VEGE-
TALES VARIEDADES AL VAPOR, POR
FAVOR.
GRACIAS.

No oil, no salt, no sugar.
Especially no MSG.
Assorted steamed vegetables, please.

Thank you.

HOW TO ORDER YOUR PRITIKIN-CHINESE MEAL
(show this to your waiter)

No oil, no salt,
no sugar.
Especially
no MSG.
Assorted
steamed
vegetables, please.
Thank you.

HOW TO ORDER YOUR PRITIKIN-FRENCH MEAL
(show this to your waiter)

PAS D'HUILE, PAS DE SEL, PAS DE
SUCRE. SURTOUT PAS DE MONO-
SODIUM GLUTAMATE. BEAUCOUP
DE LÉGUMES CUITS À LA VAPEUR,
S'IL VOUS PLAÎT.
MERCI BEAUCOUP.

No oil, no salt, no sugar.
Especially no MSG.
Assorted steamed vegetables, please.

Thank you.

HOW TO ORDER YOUR
PRITIKIN-ITALIAN MEAL
(show this to your waiter)

SENZA OLIO, SENZA SALE, SENZA ZUCCHERO. SPECIALMENTE SENZA "MSG." VERDURA MISTA A VAPORE, PER FAVORE. GRAZIE.

No oil, no salt, no sugar.
Especially no MSG.
Assorted steamed vegetables, please.

Thank you.

HOW TO ORDER YOUR
PRITIKIN-ISRAELI MEAL
(show this to your waiter)

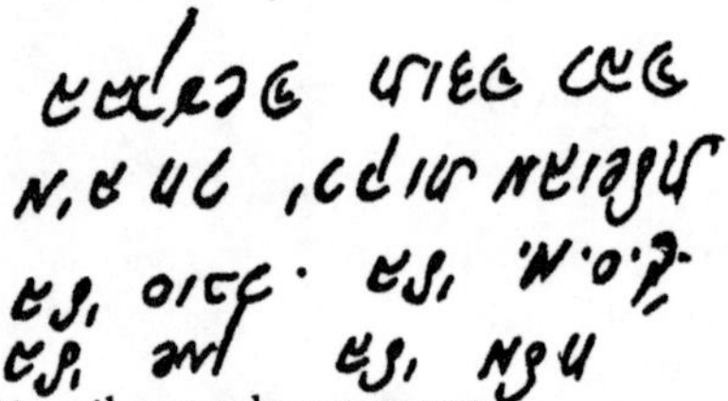

No oil, no salt, no sugar.
Especially no MSG.
Assorted steamed vegetables, please.

Thank you.

HOW TO ORDER YOUR
PRITIKIN-GERMAN MEAL
(show this to your waiter)

KEIN ÖL, SALZ, ODER ZUCKER. BESONDERS KEIN GLUTAMAT. EINE AUSWAHL DER GEDÜNSTENEN GEMÜSE BITTE.
DANKE.

No oil, no salt, no sugar.
Especially no MSG.
Assorted steamed vegetables, please.

Thank you.

France
Along the Diet Route

Three months before my husband and I were to leave for a month-long trip to France, his doctor put him on a diet that seemed insultingly anti-gallic—the rigid, highly restrictive Pritikin regimen. Len's problem was an abnormally high cholesterol level, sometimes considered a precursor of heart disease. After only a month on the program, his cholesterol level had dropped so dramatically that there seemed to be no alternative but to stay with it. I joined him for the sake of convenience and in the hope of shedding a few pounds, but gave myself license to cheat.

On the Pritikin diet, protein is limited and fats, salt, sugar, chemical additives and caffeine are strictly forbidden. That means no foods containing egg yolks, cream, butter or oil—not even the polyunsaturated kind. No red meats, almost no fish or fowl. No sweets, coffee, tea or alcohol. How could one travel in France—or anywhere, for that matter—on such a diet?

The doctor suggested that it might be wise to defer the rambling journey we had planned from Paris to Provence. His doubts were more firmly echoed by our family and friends. What fun, they asked, is a vacation that is going to be a problem three times a day? And why France, of all places, if you cannot really eat?

We seriously considered postponement. But we wanted to go, and we did. Now, we can offer some advice of our own to anyone on a diet who is contemplating a visit to France—and that takes in those who are just trying to lose or maintain weight, as well as those who are under doctor's orders. In a word: Go!

As it turned out, our trip was—with apologies to Mr. Pritikin—a piece of cake.

Our travel preparations were in no way influenced by our dietary needs. Rather, we planned our itinerary to include places both fondly remembered and new to us—a route that would take us from Paris to the chateau country, thence to Lyon via the Rhône Valley and once again to Paris. Though we intended these plans to be flexible, we rented a car and made hotel reservations in advance—a wise precaution, as it happened, even off season. We provided ourselves with a

Source: *The New York Times,* September 28, 1980. © 1980 by The New York Times Company. Reprinted by permission.

small package of diet crackers, raw vegetables and fruit to see us through the plane trip and the first few hours abroad; other than that, we planned to live off the land.

In Paris we stayed at the Angleterre, a small, moderately priced hotel on the Rue Jacob, midway between the Boulevard St. Germain and the Seine. This is the Latin Quarter, a neighborhood dominated by the university, art galleries, bookshops, antique stores—and food markets. On the Pritikin diet, light meals and lots of snacks in between are not only recommended but mandatory. We became marketers.

Each morning we joined the crowd at an open-air market on the Rue de Buci, a couple of blocks from our hotel, and filled our string bags with snacks and often provisions for a picnic lunch. Crisp, tangy beans; mushrooms; tiny, sweet tomatoes; the delicate, bud-like radishes that the French eat with butter; peas so tender you can eat the shell; baby zucchini; lettuce, cucumber, endive—the choice was endless. I was tempted by the strawberry tarts that sat invitingly in every patisserie window, but after one such indulgence found that I preferred the fresh strawberries that were mounded two feet high on the carts in the marketplace. We both became enamored of the miniature gold melons, of apricots that truly melt in the mouth and of cherries, raspberries, tender peaches and oranges that taste unlike any of the American mass-produced varieties.

Breakfast was thus easily managed with a pot of boiling water provided by the hotel and our larder of tea—linden tea, the only such beverage permitted to us, is widely available in France—fruit, and crackers and cereal from a "dietetique," the French equivalent of our health-food stores. Picnic lunches, which we preferred whenever the weather and locale were agreeable, were also taken care of. But it was restaurant meals that provided the variety and creativity that make dining in France such a delightful experience.

The streets surrounding our hotel were lined with the kind of restaurants we enjoy most—small family-owned establishments that cater to a regular neighborhood clientele and whose specialties are whatever seems best at the market that morning. We made our choices by peeking in after examining the menu that, according to law, must be posted outside the premises. If the menu devoted a special little corner to "legumes," we knew the restaurant regarded vegetables as more than an adornment. Not once were we disappointed, nor did we ever have trouble obtaining what Len required.

At La Petite Seine, a busy little restaurant with low beamed ceilings, candlelight and glass doors opening onto the quiet Rue du Pré-aux-Clercs, we were greeted on a second visit by the patron who not only remembered us but recalled exactly the requirements of Len's diet. That our bill came to about half what the average diner paid—$15, including wine for me—in no way altered the hospitality of our hosts. This was true both for the modest bistros we favored most of the time and for the luxury establishments at which we splurged on occasion.

It is possible, we discovered, to be pampered in the elegant garden setting of Ledoyen for $40 (for two). Len ordered an assiette assortie, an *hors d'oeuvre* that included julienned strips of beetroot and celeriac, a puree of carrot and salsify, radishes, small white beans and a mince of mushrooms, pepper and scallions garnished with tarragon and lemon. I had one of the specialties—caviar accompanied by a small fish similar to a sardine but less oily. From a harvest of vegetable dishes we chose some favorites rarely available on our side of the Atlantic—fat white asparagus; extra-fine crisp baby green beans flavored with chervil and dill, leeks glazed in an essence of vegetable stock and olive-shaped steamed potatoes rolled in fresh herbs. For dessert, a huge bowl of raspberries, more than we could consume in a week.

Outside of Paris, we fared even better. When we planned to eat several meals at an inn or hotel where we were staying for a few days, my husband spoke to the chef upon our arrival and then left the menu to him.

At Le Bon Laboureur in Chenonceau, in the heart of the Loire Valley, the young chef would come into the dining room while we were having a drink. He carried a basket of freshly picked vegetables for our approval; they would come back braised, baked, steamed or pureed, fragrant with newly snipped herbs, color intact and taste and textures new and delicious. Our dinners for three days cost us less than $75, including wine and numerous liters of mineral water.

Chenonceau is perhaps the most beautiful chateau setting of all—its castle spanning the Cher River, banked by woods on one side and formal gardens on the other. A road surrounded by woods leads to a park which opens on the castle. Here, nestled in the grounds, is a small building, architecturally in keeping with the setting, which houses a tearoom. Meals are served cafeteria style, but the simple fare is varied and appetizing; our salad and vegetable luncheon was $6 for two, and was Pritikin-perfect.

From Chenonceau, we followed the Loire, visiting other chateaus on the way—among them Ussé, said to be the inspiration for the story of the Sleeping Beauty, and Chambord, the largest and most lavish, with its great round towers and spectacular double spiral staircase. We stopped for a picnic lunch at Sancerre, a fortified medieval town renowned for its wines that perches in an aerie-like crown on top of a mountain. The view was enchanting, encompassing woods, vineyards, distant doll-size villages and the ribbon of the Loire.

Lyon, the commercial center of France, has for 2,000 years been a social and cultural capital; today, vestiges of the Roman capital of Gaul, the totally preserved Renaissance city of Vieux Lyon and the modern urban community sit side by side surrounded by mountains, plains and the great vineyards of Beaujolais and the Côte du Rhône.

Lyonnaise cuisine is reputed to be the finest in France. Of the 19 establishments in the whole of France awarded the coveted Michelin rating of three stars, three—Paul Bocuse, Alain Chapel and La Pyramide—are within a five-mile radius of the city proper. One- and two-star restaurants are too numerous to mention.

Many visitors to France consider dining at Paul Bocuse's restaurant at Collognes-au-Mont d'Or an experience as artistically rewarding as a tour of the Louvre. They think nothing of traveling hundreds of miles for one meal there. We had called ahead to make Len's particular needs known, a courtesy that restaurants of this caliber appreciate—and which inevitably results in a superior performance. On this occasion we splurged to the extent of including a month's ration of nonvegetable protein and feasted on flaky pike-perch, a delicate white fish that breeds in the waters of the Saône, Bresse chicken with truffles, those flavorful white beans called flageolets, dandelion salad and raspberry sherbet. Masterpieces, of course, do not come cheap; the bill was $50 a person.

From Lyon we drove south to the Route de Napoléon, a precarious but breathtaking alpine road that runs from Grenoble to Nice. Though the distance is only 200 miles, traveling is necessarily slow, since the road is a series of hairpin turns that lead up, down and around one mountain after another. The wise traveler would do well to make this a two-day journey; we, unwisely, drove all day, stopping only for a picnic lunch, until we reached Haut-de-Cagnes, one of the fortified medieval villages that dot the foothills of the Alps along the Riviera. Like its better-known neighbor, St. Paul de Vence, Haut-de-Cagnes rises almost vertically on the side of the mountain facing the Mediterranean. Our choice of this obscure village was dictated by the availability of accommodations at Le Cagnard, a multi-level inn as old as the village itself, and by the proximity to Nice, Cannes and two of the region's greatest art attractions, the Fondation Maeght in St. Paul and, in nearby Vence, the Chapelle du Rosaire, decorated by Matisse.

We had thought that the South of France, the Côte d'Azur and Provence, might pose a dietary problem. Olives and avocados are, for Pritikinites, the only forbidden fruits—and this is the land of the olive. What, we wondered, could one substitute for ratatouille, fragrant with olive oil? What could take the place of a salade Niçoise, garnished with olives and olive-oil vinaigrette? And could anyone resist the tapinade, that marvelous paste of crushed olives that is eaten with butter and crusty French bread?

But à la provençale, we soon realized, also means made with tomatoes, garlic, onions, peppers and the aromatic herbs that grow wild on the sunny hills. Though the products of the sea and mutton and wild game from the mountains are used for many local recipes, the mainstays of this cuisine are vegetables and fruit. At Les Oliviers, for example, just outside the ramparts of St. Paul de Vence, we enjoyed meatless stews and pastas exquisitely sauced with tomatoes, basil and other herbs, tangy artichokes sprinkled with lemon and the meaty white asparagus that is indigenous to France.

Provence and the Côte d'Azur are resort areas, and it was here that we encountered French culinary innovation at its best—perhaps because the local chefs are accustomed to catering to a variety of imported ailments as well as the classically French afflictions of the liver. At Le Prieuré, a converted abbey in Villeneuve-lès-Avignon, the chef prided himself on his knowledge of diets for all known conditions. Ours was new to him but afforded no difficulty. He managed to blend the flavors of basil, tomato, onion, pepper, eggplant, zucchini and garlic beautifully without oil. Salads appeared mounded with matchsticks of barely cooked lightly chilled vegetables, subtly flavored with tarragon, basil, rosemary, fennel, wild thyme and other herbs we could not identify. No sauce was needed to enjoy the garden-sweet raw vegetables that were served each evening before dinner. Whenever possible we ordered rice, a variety grown only in the Camargue and never exported, with a flavor so distinctive that no seasoning was required or desired. With wine, our dinner checks averaged $35.

We found a knowledge of French helpful in making our special needs known—particularly on the road—but we could have managed without it. At every hotel and at most restaurants at least one member of the staff and often fellow patrons spoke English; even without a common language, a dictionary and written instructions (which you can have typed up at almost any government tourist office) would have done the trick.

We have always been puzzled by tales of French rudeness

or lack of friendliness to Americans; our experiences in France have been unfailingly agreeable, and never more so than on our Pritikin-plan trip. On more than one occasion, when we unwittingly appeared at a restaurant during the hours when the kitchen was closed, the proprietor prepared something for us himself. On our swing back to Paris, we stopped at a restaurant called L'Auberge du Vieux Brancion in the Burgundian village of Brancion. We were welcomed with handshakes by both the proprietors and the few customers at the bar and were served a banquet. Villagers who stopped by for a drink or to visit with our hosts introduced themselves, asked about our travels and offered advice. We were sent off with hugs and more handshakes.

Our trip convinced us that dietary restrictions can be dealt with with surprising ease. We both returned home slimmer, healthier and more energetic than we were when we left; though poorer in pocket, we feel enriched in every other way.

6

A Practical Course in Menu Literacy

*N*ow that you have become familiar with the Pritikin diet guidelines and know some of the basics of ordering in restaurants, it's time to turn to some actual sample menus.

The menus presented in this chapter will enable you to test your own skills in choosing Pritikin-style food in a variety of situations. You can then match your selections with our recommendations as provided in the commentary regarding each menu.

Solarium

6444 Tanque Verde
Tucson, Arizona
(602) 886-8186

The Fresh Catch

The Solarium proudly features "THE FRESH CATCH."
Fresh fish selections are available, depending on
the season and the Fisherman's Luck.
SALMON • HALIBUT • PACIFIC SNAPPER
SWORDFISH • SOLE
(consult your server about today's Fresh Catch and price)

On the Light Side

Almond Chicken Salad *boned chicken with mushrooms, tomato, egg, avocado and cucumbers, topped with roasted almonds and a special dressing* — $5.95

Chef Salad *sliced ham, turkey breast, Swiss and Cheddar on a bed of mixed greens* — $4.25

Shrimp Salad *a mound of chilled select gulf shrimp with your choice of dressing* — $4.95

Seafood Salad *chilled scallops, gulf shrimp and king crab meat, served on mixed greens with vinaigrette dressing* — $5.50

Diet Plate *select top-choice ground beef surrounded by cucumbers, tomatoes with a choice of fruit salad, cottage cheese or yogurt* — $3.95

Avocado w/Shrimp *specially selected whole avocado with chilled gulf shrimp with our House Dressing (SEASONAL)* — $5.25

Tomato w/Chicken Salad *our special chicken salad with tomato and your choice of cottage cheese, yogurt or fruit salad* — $4.25

Fruit and Melon Plate *types depend on season, with a choice of cottage cheese or yogurt* — $4.25

Artichoke w/Shrimp *a California artichoke with chilled gulf shrimp, vinaigrette dressing and your choice of cottage cheese, yogurt or fruit salad (SEASONAL)* — $5.25

Chicken Salad Sandwich *our special chicken salad served on a croissant, with a choice of cottage cheese, yogurt or fruit salad* — $4.50

Scallops *tender scallops baked with garlic butter and Parmesan cheese, served on a bed of rice* — $6.50

Chef's Special

*Each day at the Solarium something special and
uniquely different is offered for lunch.*

Ask Your Server About Today's Selection

Calamari *lightly breaded and pan fried, served abalone* $5.25
style with garlic butter

Chicken Teriyaki *boneless chicken breast marinated in* $4.95
teriyaki sauce, served on a bed of rice

Top Sirloin *Midwestern top choice steak, broiled to your* $6.50
order

*Entrées: includes choice of soup of the day, seafood chowder
or salad, vegetable or steak fries*

Solarium Sandwich *roasted prime rib and cheddar* $4.95
cheese grilled on sourdough bread

Monte Cristo *turkey breast, ham, Swiss and Cheddar* $4.50
cheese grilled on toast with a light egg batter

Bacon, Lettuce, Tomato and Avocado $3.95
need we say more?

French Dip *roasted prime rib, sliced thin, on a French* $4.95
roll, au jus

Club Sandwich *triple decker, sliced breast of turkey, crisp* $3.95
bacon, sliced tomatoes and iceberg lettuce

Super Burger *Midwestern top choice ground beef with* $3.95
lettuce, pickles, onion and tomato

Sandwich Board: served with soup of the day and steak fries

Extras		**Desserts**	
Seafood Chowder	$2.25	Strawberry Shortcake	$2.25
Sautéed Mushrooms	$1.75	Cheese Cake	$1.95
Artichoke (Hot or Cold)	$2.75	With Strawberries	$2.50
French-Fried Artichoke		Strawberries Supreme	$2.50
Hearts (Seasonal)	$3.50	Bananas Supreme	$2.50
Soup and Dinner Salad	$3.95		
Extra Plate	$2.00		

Beverages

Iced Tea, Hot Tea, Coffee, Milk

Coffee Shop

"Coffee shop" is a loose term. The Solarium, whose menu is shown on pages 82–83, is a beautiful restaurant with a very obliging management, but we used "Coffee Shop" as the heading because many of the menu items tend to be the kind you might find in such establishments. Items featured include bacon, lettuce, and tomato sandwiches, club sandwiches, superburgers, and the misnamed "diet plate"—a ground beef patty with cottage cheese, fruit salad, or yogurt, and a few raw vegetables. This "diet plate" is very high in fat, cholesterol, and protein especially because of the ground beef patty—hardly suitable fare for you.

Some of the salads on this menu would be wrong choices, mainly because of the mayonnaise (eggs and oil form the base) or other oil-based dressings already mixed into them. This would not be the case with the fruit-and-melon plate, but the cottage cheese or yogurt accompanying it would probably not be the fat-free variety. If you order this plate, ask for additional fruit as a substitute for the cottage cheese or yogurt, and ask the waiter to serve it to you with some of the restaurant's sourdough bread. The chef's salad is another possibility, but have the ham and the two cheeses left off, and ask the waiter to substitute additional turkey breast or other vegetables. You might order the seafood salad, but it would need modification. Since crab and shrimp are both high-cholesterol shellfish, you need to watch your intake of them. Ask to have the salad served to you with a minimum of crab and shrimp—or better yet, with only scallops (a low-cholesterol shellfish). As a substitute, ask for additional vegetables. And request a wedge of lemon or wine vinegar instead of the oily vinaigrette dressing.

None of the sandwich selections are acceptable in the manner they are usually prepared. But you could ask to have the chef custom-make you a sandwich using, for example, sourdough bread, white meat of turkey, lettuce, tomato, and onions. If you like, put a little mustard on the bread, or leave the bread dry.

Under "Extras," you might want to order the artichoke, which happens to be the lowest-calorie item on the menu. Hot or cold and with a little lemon juice squeezed over it, an artichoke is a delicacy. Seafood chowder, whether Boston (or New England) cream-style or the Manhattan tomato-style, usually is not acceptable, because of the use of such ingredients as butter, possibly salt pork, and, in the case of the Boston chowder, cream.

If you want to order the fish, ask to have it broiled without fat or butter, or have it poached. Though not listed on the menu, baked potatoes are available here, and you could have one to accompany your fish. Or, ask to have the fish served to you with some of the rice that is offered with the chicken teriyaki. That dish, too, might be a possibility if the teriyaki sauce has little or no oil in it and contains minimal soy sauce.

The fresh strawberries would make a delightful meal ending.

The Original
Seafood Broiler
Seafood Restaurant & Market

11701-A Wilshire Blvd.
Brentwood, CA
(213) 473-1551

1199 No. Euclid
Anaheim, CA
(714) 778-5000

5545 Reseda Blvd.
Tarzana, CA
(213) 996-0100

12743 Ventura Blvd.
Studio City, CA
(213) 766-8131

919 South Central
Glendale, CA
(213) 243-1195

4333 Candlewood St.
Lakewood, CA
(213) 634-3474

620 Pacific Coast Hwy.
Seal Beach, CA
(213) 594-9444

8600 Van Nuys Blvd.
Panorama City, CA
(213) 891-5602

21233 Hawthorne Blvd.
Torrance, CA
(213) 316-3133

17601 Castleton St.
City Of Industry, CA
(213) 965-5112

735 E. Green St.
Pasadena, CA
(213) 795-9755

12892 Harbor Blvd.
Garden Grove, CA
(714) 638-9500

For Starters
Appetizers • Cocktails

Shrimp—Small Size	3.25
Shrimp—Large Size	4.25
Crabmeat	3.95
Crab & Small Shrimp	3.75
Crab & Large Shrimp	3.95
Oyster Cocktail	2.75
Clam Cocktail	3.25

*Served with a Special
Sauce and Fresh Lemon*

FRESH
CLAMS 'N' OYSTERS

*Steamed Clams with Clam
Broth and Melted Butter*
Small 4.25   Large 5.25

Clams *fresh on the half shell
—Served Chilled—*

Oysters *fresh on the half shell
—Served Chilled—*

Combination *¹/₂ Clams and
¹/₂ Oysters on the half shell
—Served Chilled—*

*All served with our Special
Sauce and Fresh Lemon*

Light Combinations

*Includes a Bowl of our Clam
Chowder—A Large Dinner
Salad—Hot Roll & Butter
$2.95
Add: Any Small Order of Clams
or Oysters, Steamed or
Half-Shell or a Small Smoked
Fish Plate $5.95*

Smoked Fish
Appetizer Plate

*Served with Fresh Lemon
and our Special Sauce*
Small 3.75   Large 4.75

*Our own Famous
Boston Style*
Clam Chowders
(White) $1.60

Manhattan Style
Clam Chowders
(Red) $1.60
*Add Hot Sourdough
Roll and Butter $1.75*

Ask our waitress about the entrées that meet the Dietary Guidelines set by the American Heart Association.

All fish entrées may be cooked without seasoning, butter or oil.

House diet dressing, margarine, non-dairy creamer, and salt substitute available upon request.

---

*Fresh Ripe Tomato
(Stuffed with Our Tasty)*
Fish Salad

A bowl of
Clam Chowder
*Roll and Butter—Coffee, Tea
Milk or Soft Drink
$4.50*

Soup & Shrimp Salad Supreme

*Includes a bowl of Clam Chowder with our finest Bay Shrimp on mixed greens, choice of dressing and hot sourdough roll and butter.
$6.50
no substitutions

Salads

Seafood Salad	6.75
Topped with Shrimp and Crab Meat	
Stuffed Tomato	2.95
Fresh Tomato Stuffed with Tasty Fish Salad Served on Mixed Greens	
Crab Salad	6.95
Fruit & Cottage Cheese Salad	3.95
Shrimp/Avocado	5.95
One Half Avocado Stuffed with Bay Shrimp	
Shrimp Salad	5.95
Small-Sized Shrimp	
Shrimp Salad	8.50
Large-Sized Shrimp	
Crab & Large-Sized Shrimp Salad	7.75
Tuna/Avocado One	4.95
Half Avocado Stuffed with White Meat Tuna	
Stuffed Tomato & Tuna Salad	4.95

All Above Served with Choice of Dressing, Sourdough Roll and Butter

Beverages

Coffee	.60
Milk	.60
Hot Tea	.60
Iced Tea	.60
Coke, 7-Up, Tab	.60
Sanka	.60

Side Orders

Dinner Salad	*Sm .95*	*Lg 1.50*
Sourdough Roll		.35
Cherry Tomatoes		.85
Our Own Potatoes		.85
Cole Slaw		.85
Sweet Corn		.85
Salad Dressing		.85
Rice Pilaf		.85

Blackboard Specialties

Pacific Red Snapper	6.75
California Pacific Oysters	6.95
Mahi Mahi	6.95
Yellowtail	6.95
Ocean Cod Filet	6.95
Eastern Haddock	6.95
Shark	6.95

Combination Fish   8.25
  Kabob *Shrimp, Scallops,
  Select Cuts of Fish, Spaced
  with Onions and Bell Peppers*
Catfish *Farm grown.*   7.95
  A real delicacy
Shrimp *on a skewer,*   9.50
  *spaced w/bacon, served
  w/melted butter*
Scallops *on a skewer,*   8.75
  *spaced w/bacon, sweet
  in flavor*
Shrimp and Scallops   8.95
  *Delectable Shrimp and
  Scallops on a skewer,
  spaced w/bacon, natural
  wood broiled*
Salmon   8.95
  North Pacific's Finest
Halibut *North Filet,*   8.75
  Natural Wood Broiled
Swordfish *"A Seafood*   9.25
  *Delight." Natural
  Wood Broiled*
Cracked Crab *Sweet*   8.25
  *& Tender, Served chilled
  w/special sauce*
Lobster, Shrimp and   12.95
  Scallops *Sampler of
  Shellfish on a skewer, spaced
  w/onion, bell peppers,
  natural wood broiled*
King Crab *Rich 'n*   14.95
  *flavor, Broiled in shell
  w/melted butter*
Lobster *House*   14.95
  *delicacy, served on a
  skewer w/melted butter*

EAT FISH
"LIVE LONGER"

"SHORE DINNER"

*Fresh Water Trout . . . Broiled
A Large Boneless Trout Cooked
Over an Open Fire to
Perfection*
6.95

"A House Favorite"
Eastern Scrod
5.95
*Delicate & Moist
Natural Wood Broiled
To a tender goodness*

Ocean Perch
5.95
*Tender, mild & flaky
White Meat Filet
A Fish Eater's Delight*

Subject to Availability

Child's Plates
*on a skewer
(12 and UNDER ONLY)*

Shrimp Skewer	4.95
Fish—*Select Cuts*	3.95
Halibut—*Select Cuts*	3.95

TRY ONE OF OUR
DELICIOUS DESSERTS

CHECK OUR WINE LIST

Seafood Restaurant

Among the most popular kinds of restaurants are those serving seafoods. They're usually good choices because fish, if it's prepared properly, tends to be lower in fat and cholesterol than meat. And fish lends itself well to baking, broiling without oil or butter, steaming, or poaching or sautéing in wine, stock, or water with lemon juice.

The menu on pages 86–88 comes from the Seafood Broiler, a family-type seafood restaurant chain in California. From the "Side Orders," you can tell at a glance what the situation is with respect to your chances of getting enough complex-carbohydrate foods. The rice doesn't look promising because of the method of preparation, and the potatoes are probably fried, but you could verify this with your waiter or waitress. On the positive side, you could certainly order several sweet corns (unbuttered) and have a few sourdough rolls. Select a dinner salad too (ask for a wedge of lemon) and/or the cherry tomatoes. Don't order the cole slaw, though, if it has a creamy dressing.

Under "Salads," shrimp and crab are prominently featured. Both are very high in cholesterol, so if you order a seafood salad (or appetizer) with shrimp or crabmeat or both, the portion needs to be *half* your usual 3½-ounce-per-day total allotment for poultry, seafood, and meat. (Clams, scallops, oysters, and lobster are all permitted on the usual allotment basis.) Another complication with the salads is that frequently the dressings are already mixed in; you'll need to ask if this is the case. Avocado is featured in some of the salads and needs to be avoided, as it's extremely high in fat. (Foods derived from plants, in general, are very low in fat, but avocados, olives, nuts, and sunflower seeds—all favorite salad ingredients—are not permitted on the Pritikin diet.)

Don't get discouraged, though. This menu has lots of possibilities. Bypass the seafood chowder because of the cream, salt, and other no-no's, and head straight for the fish selections. This restaurant will broil your selection without fats, upon request. Ask whether a little lemon juice (and/or wine) can be used instead. Another interesting possibility is the lobster, shrimp, and scallop skewer with vegetables, which could also be broiled with a little lemon juice and would be acceptable if there were lots of vegetables and not too much shrimp on the skewer.

The special "health" offerings of margarine, nondairy creamer, and house diet dressing are all "no, thank you" items, since all have oil bases. As to a salt substitute, most of them contain substances such as potassium chloride that can be harmful, particularly to those with hypertension.

The Cypress

(Mr. Sean Hartney, Mgr.)
500 East Ogden
Hinsdale, IL 60521
(312) 323-2727

Appetizers

Cocktail of Jumbo Shrimps (per shrimp)	1.50	Baked Shrimps DeJonghe en Petite Casserole	4.95
Blue Points on the Half Shell	3.95	Mushrooms Rockefeller, Mushroom caps broiled in butter and Blue Cheese	2.25
		(for two)	3.95

Soups

Soup du Jour	Cup .95	Bowl 1.75	
French Onion, Cheese Croutons	Cup .95	Bowl 1.75	

Seafood

Broiled Filet of Florida Red Snapper, Almondine Butter — 12.95

Shrimps DeJonghe, Firm selected tender shrimps are sautéed in butter, garlic and Sherry wine, crowned with slices of DeJonghe butter and baked to a golden brown — 11.95

Sautéed Sea Scallops, Tartar or Cocktail Sauce — 9.95

Whole Dover Sole, Sautéed, then baked golden brown, boned at your table, Almondine Butter — Mkt.

Broiled Lobster Tail, Large and meaty, served on the shell with plenty of Drawn butter — 1 Tail Mkt. 2 Tails Mkt.

Combinations

Ship and Shore, Broiled Lobster Tail with Drawn Butter and a Conservative Cut Filet Mignon — Mkt.

Surf and Turf, Broiled Florida Red Snapper, Almondine Butter and Conservative Cut Top Sirloin Butt Steak — 13.50

Beef

Roast Prime Rib of Beef

Tenderly roasted cut of aged Blue Ribbon Beef,
served in its own natural juices
with our own Horseradish Bernaise Sauce
11.95   Extra-Thick Cut   14.95

Broiled Filet Mignon, Sauce Bernaise — 13.95
Conservative Cut — 10.95

Broiled Top Sirloin Butt Steak, Sauce Bernaise — 11.95
Conservative Cut — 8.95

90

Broiled New York Cut Sirloin Steak,   *13.95*
Sauce Bernaise   Conservative Cut   *10.95*

London Broil, *Sliced seasoned flank steak, Bordelaise*   *8.95*
Sauce

Chateaubriand *(for two or more), Garnished with potato rosettes, broiled tomato, broccoli spears, baby carrots, French fried onion rings, mushrooms and asparatus spears. Sauce Bernaise*   Per Couple   *30.00*

Specialties of the House

Sautéed Veal, *Extraordinarily tender medallions of milk-fed veal from the strip loin, lightly sautéed in lemon butter and wine, and served with asparagus spears*   *13.95*

Mediterranean Braised Lamb Shank, *Braised in fresh lemon, olive oil, spices, herbs, and Velouté Sauce à la Cypress*   *9.95*

Calves Liver, *Sautéed in butter and served with mushrooms, onions, peppers and bacon*   *10.95*

Southern Style Hickory Barbecued Ribs, *Tender and meaty back ribs with our own special honey sauce*   *12.95*

Boston Scrod, *Lightly coated with seasoned bread crumbs, baked to a golden brown and served with Tartar Sauce*   *10.95*

Pepper Steak à la Cypress, *Slices of beef tenderloin sautéed in butter, served with mushrooms, onions, green peppers and tomatoes. Burgundy Sauce, wild rice Cypress style*   *10.95*

Specialties of the Day

Each day our chefs prepare from one to three additional specialties for the evening meal.
Your waitress will be happy to describe them to you.
We recommend them highly!

Salads

Cypress Garden Salad Plate, with choice of dressing
(included with entrée)
Green Goddess or Blue Cheese Dressing .65 extra

Spinach Salad, *A delightful taste blend of fresh spinach, bacon, red onions, chopped egg and our own special dressing*   *2.95*
          (for two)   *4.95*

Caesar Salad   *2.95*
          (for two)   *4.95*

Vegetables

French Fried Potatoes   Baked Potato   Whipped Potato
or Vegetable du Jour
(included with entrée)

Fresh Sautéed Mushrooms	1.95	Broccoli or Asparagus	1.75
Wild Rice Cypress Style	1.25	with Hollandaise	2.50
Hash Browned Potatoes	1.50	Stuffed Baked Potato	1.25

Beverages

Coffee	.65	Selection of Teas	.65
Milk	.65	Fresh Brewed	
		Decaffeinated Coffee	.65

The Fine Dinner Restaurant

The dinner menu on pages 90–92 is from the type of restaurant you're apt to frequent with business associates, relatives, or friends from out of town, because it offers fare that is not overly spicy and that most people are comfortable with. Though a first glance at the menu may make you think you're unlikely to find a Pritikin-type meal at this establishment, this is actually not so. Furthermore, the owner of this restaurant caters to Pritikin diners and will prepare to your specifications many entrées and side dishes not listed on the menu.

But let's suppose that this is not the case and that you are ordering just on the basis of what is offered on the menu. If you wanted to start with a soup, the French onion soup wouldn't qualify because the onions are sautéed in butter, the soup is usually quite salty, and, for good measure, cheese croutons are sprinkled on top. Ask about the soup du jour. It might be acceptable.

If you are going to choose a seafood, beef, or other animal-food entrée, it would be best not to have one of the shellfish appetizers, since you need to concern yourself with staying within your total daily animal-food limit of 3½ ounces.

The "Seafood" section would be a good place from which to select your entrée. How about red snapper or lobster tail, broiled without butter or oil, but basted with a little lemon juice? The scallops and the sole, sautéed in lemon juice and water or white wine and water, would also be good choices. Ask your waiter or waitress to leave the butter in the kitchen and to bring you plenty of lemon wedges instead. And with the scallops, you could also use the cocktail sauce.

The London broil would be the least fatty beef choice. Ask for Dijon mustard or some uncreamed horseradish instead of the Bordelaise sauce. Among the "Specialties of the House," the choices are nil because of the high-fat and/or high-cholesterol content of the meats, or the style of preparation in the case of the Boston scrod. The chef may be willing to adapt the scrod recipe to Pritikin guidelines by using unbuttered bread crumbs, egg white only, if egg is used to adhere the crumbs to the fish, and so on. If he does Pritikinize the recipe for you, ask to have the fish served with lemon wedges or cocktail sauce, instead of the mayonnaise-based Tartar sauce. Ask about the "Specialties of the Day," however. (At this restaurant, chicken breast will be cooked without skin, upon request.)

Round out your meal with a baked potato and the garden salad plate. Don't choose the spinach salad, not only because it contains chopped egg and bacon bits (which are taboo regardless of whether they're real or made with soy), but also because spinach is not a preferred vegetable. That's because it contains oxalates which prevent the absorption of calcium and other minerals. It's okay to eat small amounts of spinach occasionally, but not with these accompaniments.

If you like, ask whether the chef will steam asparagus or broccoli, or perhaps sauté in wine some mushrooms or a green vegetable.

Make sure you stay within the limits for your daily animal-food allotment. Share a serving with a dinner partner or carry the excess home in a doggy bag, as you prefer.

The Artful Balance

525½ North Fairfax Avenue
Los Angeles, CA 90036
(213) 852-9091

Changing Daily

*Consult the Table Card for
Today's Flavor of*
Fresh Fish
*includes rice or potato
or 1 steamed vegetable*
Poultry
Vegetarian Entrées
Chef's Option
Soups
cup 2.00   *bowl* 3.50
Sauce   2.00
Beans   3.00
Desserts

Hot Food

½ Roast Chicken   8.00
*Roasted with no flour or oil.
Served with your choice of
brown rice or ½ baked po-
tato or 1 steamed vegetable*
Broiled Pacific Red   8.00
Snapper *(seasonal) Fresh
filet, plain or fancy. Served
with your choice of brown
rice or ½ baked potato or
1 steamed vegetable*
Vegetable Stew   *Fresh*   7.00
*vegetables in a great herbed
sauce, no dairy products*
Hot Artichoke   4.00
*(seasonal)   With mayon-
naise or drawn butter*

More Hot Food

Vegetarian Chili   *Delicious & hearty combination
of beans, mushrooms, vegetables & mild spices*
cup	4.00
cup with cheese	4.50
bowl	7.00
bowl with cheese	8.00
chili over rice	6.50
chili over rice	
with cheese	7.50

Tostada Superior   7.00
*Crisp corn tortilla topped
with beans, vegetarian chili,
salad, guacamole, cheese
and sauce*
Sautéed Vegetables   7.00
*Thinly sliced onion, carrot,
broccoli, cauliflower, and
summer squashes, stir-fried in
a wok with garlic, olive oil
and tamari*
Sautéed with Tofu   8.00
Steamed Vegetables   6.00
*Broccoli, cauliflower, car-
rots, and summer squashes*
½ Order Steamed	
Vegetables	4.00
Melted Cheese on Top	1.75
Steamed Brown Rice	
cup	1.25
bowl	1.75
Steamed Tofu	2.00
Baked Potato	2.50

Table Condiments   *Sea salt,
cayenne, tamari*
Also Available   *honey, chop-
sticks, sesame salt, black pepper, spike, cinnamon*

95

Cold Food

Garden Medley Salad
Basic tossed green assortment of Romaine and salad bowl lettuce, tomato, carrots, and purple cabbage and cucumber

small	2.50
large	5.50

Spinach Salad With sliced mushrooms, chopped egg, soy bacon bits and green onions

small	4.00
large	7.00

Raw Vegetables Broccoli, cauliflower, carrot, summer squash, and sprouts

side order	4.00
salad plate	7.00

French Vegetable Salad
Lightly marinated in an herbed vinaigrette, green beans, carrots, potatoes, peas, cauliflower and cucumbers

side order	4.50
salad plate	7.50

Chicken Liver Plate 6.00
Served with rye crackers, or 8.00
cucumber, tomato and onion, organic chicken liver, sherry, herbs and agar agar. Dijon mustard on the side.

Fruit Plate
(seasonal selection)

small	5.00
large	7.00

Fruit Plate
(seasonal selection)
With yogurt or cheese

small	6.00
large	8.00

More Cold Food

Curried Chicken Salad
With raisins, green onion, Jicama or Jerusalem artichoke and mayonnaise

side order	6.00
salad plate	8.00

Cold Artichoke
(seasonal) 4.00
With mayonnaise or lemon herb dressing

Guacamole 4.00
Avocado, mild chilis, onion, cilantro, tomato and lemon. With chips and cucumber slices.

Peas and Watercress With cubes of Jack cheese, roasted sunflower seeds, and tomatoes lightly marinated in lemon herb dressing

side order	4.50
salad plate	7.50

Cold Tofu	2.00
Sliced Avocado	3.00
Sliced Mushrooms	3.50
Sliced Tomato	2.00
Grated Cheese	1.75
Sour Cream	1.50
Cottage Cheese	2.00
Yogurt	2.00
Applesauce	2.00

Dressings Available
Lemon Herb
Blue Cheese
Tarragon Tahini
Sweet Vermouth Vinaigrette

Beverages

JUICES		HERB TEAS	1.00
Hot Cider with Cinnamon	2.00	Peppermint	
Apple Cider	1.50	Chamomile	
Cranberry	1.50	Rosehips	
Lemonade	1.50	Comfrey	
		Mellow Mint	
WATERS		Lemon Mist	
Calistoga or ?	1.50	Pelican Punch	
Perrier	2.00	Sleepy Time	
COFFEE	1.00	Mandarin Orange Spice	
Hot		Mo's 24	
Iced		Red Zinger	
Brewed Decaffeinated		ICED TEAS	1.00
GRAIN DRINKS	1.00	Peppermint	
Pero		Red Zinger	
Roastaroma		Regular	
MILK	1.50	BLACK TEAS	1.00
		Morning Thunder	

You are welcome to bring your own unopened wine or beer to consume with your meal. We'll open it and provide glasses.

Orange Pekoe & Pekoe
Darjeeling
Jasmine
Earl Grey

Corkage   2.50   Constant Comment

TAKEOUT PACKAGING   10%

Natural Food Restaurant

Natural or health food restaurants offer mixed blessings—a sprinkling of good selections and others that are, ironically, plain unhealthful. That's because some of the criteria that such restaurants use for good nutrition are misguided. For instance, most of these establishments serve whole grains, but it's sometimes difficult to find a dish that isn't smothered under a blanket of melted cheese, lubricated with globs of butter, or drenched in oil.

There are, however, some excellent choices on the menu from The Artful Balance (pages 95–97) if you're menu-wise. Under "More Hot Food," note the baked potato, steamed vegetables, and steamed brown rice. The vegetarian chili looks good; just order it without the cheese. Tofu is a cholesterol-free food, but since it's very high in protein and quite high in fat, it's counted as a substitute for poultry, fish, or seafood in your 3½ ounce/day total allotment. If you are fond of it, order the steamed tofu, perhaps with the steamed vegetables. If you prefer both sautéed, ask to have them sautéed in a little white wine instead of the olive oil and tamari.

You'll probably need to pass on the tostada. The tortilla is fried, guacamole is made with oil-rich avocado, and, as if that's not enough, there is cheese. But you could ask whether the chef can oven-crisp the tortilla and skip the guacamole and cheese for you.

Under "Hot Food," if the roast chicken or red snapper appeals to you, it's fine to order one of these dishes—but remember portion sizes. The roast chicken sounds as though it could feed you for a few days! Share oversize animal-food entrées with dinner partners or tote home the excess in a doggy bag. Also in that section, both the vegetable stew and the artichoke are good candidates, but have them hold the mayonnaise and the drawn butter.

The "Cold Food" and "More Cold Food" sections hold promise, but stay away from the chicken liver pâté. Liver, whether organic or inorganic, is one of the highest sources of cholesterol and contains other undesirable substances as well.

You could order the fruit plate without the yogurt or cheese, since only the nonfat variety of these dairy products is allowed. It is unlikely that you'll find nonfat dairy products served in restaurants, although it never hurts to ask. Every little bit helps in reeducating those who feed us.

If you prefer a green salad, ask for one with an accompaniment of lemon wedges or vinegar instead of one of the restaurant's dressings, which are almost always made with oil. Unfortunately, spinach salad, as explained on page 94, is not preferred Pritikin fare.

You could order the peas and watercress and ask for sliced mushrooms and tomatoes (listed further down in the same column) instead of the cheese and seeds. Some restaurant owners, chefs, waiters, and waitresses are extremely obliging and eager to please, and it never hurts to ask.

Mana Kai Maui Condominium/Hotel

2960 S. Kihei Road
Kihei, Maui, Hawaii 96753
(808) 879-2607

A SPECIAL FEATURE AT MANA KAI MAUI CONDOMINIUM/HOTEL

PRITIKIN BETTER HEALTH PROGRAM*

ALOHA

Naturally Yours

It is our pleasure to offer you the benefits and opportunities for building better health that the Pritikin diet has demonstrated in over 25 years of scientific nutritional research and successful application. Experience these delicious, wholesome natural meals high in nutritional value which are prepared without fats, oils, sugars, additives, preservatives, cholesterol, or added salts. All meals are prepared according to guidelines of Nathan Pritikin. Besides breakfast, we also offer lunch and dinner.

BREAKFAST

Naturally Sweet Juices

- Pineapple
- Apple
- Orange
- Grapefruit
- Unsalted Tomato
- Low-Sodium V-8

Pritikin-Style Herbal Brews (Caffeine-Free)

- Red Bush Tea (Plain)
- Red Bush Mint Tea
- Red Bush Orange Spice
- Chamomile Tea
- Brewed Duram Un-Coffee
- Cafix Instant Un-Coffee

Maui-Fresh Fruit

- Small Maui-Fresh Fruit Cup
- Papaya Half with lime wedge
- Pineapple Spears
- Sliced Banana (seasonal)

The Morning Grain Market

- Whole Grain Hot Cereal of the Day (Served with skim milk)

Oatmeal	Rye	Cracked Wheat
7-Grain	4-Grain	Hearts of Bran

- Crunchy Whole Grain Cereals (Cold) (Served with skim milk)
  Sprouted 7-Grain with raisins
  Nutri-Grain Corn Flakes
- Whole Wheat Pancakes
  Served with unsweetened fruit spread
- May we suggest Fruit, Applesauce, or Cinnamon as a Sweetener

---

*The use of the names "Pritikin" and "Pritikin Better Health Program" are by special arrangement with Pritikin Programs, P.O. Box 5335, Santa Barbara, CA 93108.

HEALTHY COMPLEMENTS

- *Pritikin Toast (rye or wheat)*
- *Pritikin English Muffins (above served with unsweetened fruit spread)*
- *Oven-Baked "Fries" (Kula potatoes)*
- *Skim Milk*

- *Sweet Sprouted Wheat Bread (Essene Bread) with unsweetened fruit spread*
- *Applesauce*
- *Nonfat Yogurt, Plain*
  —with Fruit
  —with Granola
  —with "The Works"

Natural Eats

9477 S. Dixie Highway
Miami, FL 33156
665-7807

BREAKFAST

Beverages

Orange Juice	.65	X-Lg.	1.05
Apple Juice	.65	X-Lg.	1.05
Coffee			.40
Tea			.40
Fresh Milk			.65

Fresh Fruits

Fresh Fruit Medley	1.95

Natural Drinks

Fruit Smoothie	1.39

(Fresh fruits & juices blended into an icy shake)

The Good Morning Breakfast (2 scrambled eggs, homemade hash browns and toasted pita bread) — 1.99

Egg in a Sack (One scrambled egg, melted cheese in pita bread, then we add our Special Sauce) — 1.40

Fresh Omelette and Cheese (Mixture of 2 eggs and cheese, your choice of vegetables, served with toasted pita bread) — 2.29

Natural T.E.C. (Tomato-Egg-Cheese) (2 scrambled eggs, tomatoes and our special cheese blend served in pita bread, lightly sprinkled with our secret dressing) — 2.00

French Toast (2 slices of whole-wheat bread dipped in an egg batter and cooked golden brown, served with natural maple syrup) — 2.99

Granola or Assorted Cereal w/Milk — 1.00

Side Orders

Bagels	
served with butter	.75
cream cheese (additional)	.35
Toasted Pita Bread	.40
Bran Muffins	.79
Skin Fries	.75
Homemade Hash Browns	.59

Breakfast Menus

The breakfast foods offered at the Mana Kai Maui (pages 100–101) are a true Pritikin dieter's treat. Although you won't often find a breakfast menu like it, we have included it to give you an idea of some of the delicious foods that could be offered—from marvelous fresh fruits to whole-grain cereals and whole-wheat pancakes, as well as numerous delicious-sounding accompaniments. Hopefully, as time goes on, more and more breakfast menus will resemble this one.

We have also included a more typical breakfast menu, from Natural Eats (page 102). The best choice on this menu would be the fresh fruit medley, accompanied by bagels or toasted pita bread served without butter. Of course, it would be best if the breads were made with whole grains, but the most important thing is to avoid the use of a fatty spread. Bran muffins sound healthful, but are generally made with eggs and with oil or butter. Commercial granola, another healthful-sounding food, is usually high in both sugar and fat.

For a more complete discussion of what to order from breakfast menus, see page 134.

Sai Wu Restaurant

109 Atlantic Street
Stamford, Connecticut

Tel. 348-3330
327-8942

Appetizers

Egg Roll (2)	1.90
Roast Pork (small)	2.60
Roast Pork (large)	5.10
Barbecued Spareribs (small)	3.95
Barbecued Spareribs (large)	7.90
Fantail Shrimp (small)	4.10
(large)	8.10
Teriyaki Beef Cubes of beef steak marinated in Tahiti style.	4.65
Dim Sum Minced pork meat with water chestnuts, wrapped in egg noodles and steamed.	1.70
Shrimp Toast	3.75
Gee Bow Gai	3.00
Chicken meat marinated in a special sauce wrapped in a golden foil.	

Soup

	Pt.	Qt.
Egg Drop Soup	1.15	2.15
Wonton Soup	1.35	2.55

Chow Mein

	Pt.	Qt.
Chow Mein	2.20	4.25
Roast Pork Chow Mein	2.20	4.25
Vegetable Chow Mein (meatless)	2.20	4.25
Beef Chow Mein	2.95	5.40
Shrimp Chow Mein	3.10	5.90
Sai Wu Chicken Chow Mein	2.70	5.15
Subgum Chicken Chow Mein	2.70	5.15
Subgum Shrimp Chow Mein	3.35	6.45
Roast Pork Chow Mein Cantonese style, soft noodle (per order)		5.95

Lo Mein

	Per Order
Beef Lo Mein (Cantonese style—soft noodle)	5.15
Roast Pork Lo Mein	4.75
Chicken Lo Mein	4.75
Fresh Shrimp Lo Mein	5.75

Chop Suey

	Pt.	Qt.
Vegetable Chop Suey (meatless)	2.15	4.20
Pork Chop Suey	2.30	4.50
Beef Chop Suey	2.80	5.35
Shrimp Chop Suey	3.10	5.80
Chicken Chop Suey	2.40	4.75
Subgum Chicken Chop Suey	2.60	5.10
Subgum Shrimp Chop Suey	3.30	6.40

Fried Rice

	Pt.	Qt.
Roast Pork Fried Rice	2.10	4.10
Shrimp or Beef Fried Rice	2.90	5.80
Chicken Fried Rice	2.20	4.30
Subgum Fried Rice	3.00	5.90
Boiled Rice	.75	1.30

Egg Foo Young
(Chinese Omelette)

	Per Order
Roast Pork Egg Foo Young	3.95
Shrimp Egg Foo Young	4.85
Chicken Egg Foo Young	4.10
Chicken Egg Foo Young, Cantonese Style	5.00
Shrimp Egg Foo Young, Cantonese Style	5.85
Roast Pork Egg Foo Young, Cantonese Style	5.00

Pork

	Pt.
Roast Pork with Bean Sprouts	2.50
Roast Pork with Chinese Vegetables	2.90
Roast Pork with Mixed Chinese Vegetables	3.10
Almond Charshu Ding (Diced Roast Pork with Snow Pea Pods, Oyster Sauce, Chinese Vegetables)	3.10
Roast Pork with Snow Pea Pods, Oyster Sauce	5.10
Sweet and Pungent Breaded Spareribs or Pork	5.25

Beef

	Pt.
Pepper Steak with Onions	3.20
Pepper Steak with Tomato	3.35
Beef with Bean Sprouts	2.80
Beef with Chinese Vegetables	3.20
Beef with Mixed Chinese Vegetables	3.40
Beef with Snow Pea Pods, Oyster Sauce	5.30

Sea Food

	Pt.
Fresh Shrimp with Bean Sprouts	3.20
Fresh Shrimp with Chinese Vegetables	4.50
Fresh Shrimp with Lobster Sauce (per order)	7.45
Sweet and Pungent Har Kew (shrimp)	6.45
Breaded Shrimp with Mixed Vegetables	6.85
Wor Hip Har (Butterfly Shrimp Wrapped with Bacon)	7.25
Lobster Cantonese Style (seasonal price)	

Poultry

	Pt.
Moo Goo Gai Pan White meat chicken, mushrooms, water chestnuts, bamboo shoots and vegetables	3.10
Almond Gai Ding Diced chicken, almonds and Chinese vegetables	3.10

Bo Lo Gai Pan White 3.25
meat chicken, pineapple and
Chinese vegetables

	Per Order
Breaded Boneless Chicken, Cantonese Style	5.70
Wor Shew Opp Duckling w/mushroom sauce and Chinese Vegetables	5.95
Sweet & Pungent Gai Kew Breaded chicken with sweet & sour sauce	5.75

Combination Platters

1. Chicken Chow Mein, Fried Rice & Egg Roll	4.00
2. Shrimp Chow Mein, Fried Rice & Egg Roll	5.15
3. Shrimp with Lobster Sauce, Fried Rice & Egg Roll	6.45
4. Pepper Steak, Fried Rice & Egg Roll	4.80
5. Barbecued Spareribs, Fried Rice & Egg Roll	5.75
6. Pork or Beef Chop Suey, Fried Rice & Egg Roll	4.35
7. Subgum Chicken Chow Mein, Fried Rice & Egg Roll	4.55
8. Roast Pork or Beef Bok Toy, Fried Rice & Egg Roll	4.90
9. Moo Goo Gai Pan, Fried Rice & Egg Roll	5.15
10. Lobster (half) Cantonese Style, Fried Rice & Egg Roll	7.35

Szechuan Dishes

	Per Order
Shredded Beef with Green Pepper	7.75
Baby Shrimp with Hot Pepper Sauce	8.50
Shrimp with Garlic Sauce (Sautéed with mushrooms, water chestnuts, and hot garlic sauce)	8.50
Shredded Pork with Green Peppers	6.55
Beef with Scallions	7.95

105

Beef Hunan Style   7.95
(Marinated beef sautéed with water chestnuts, mushrooms, and broccoli in hot garlic sauce)

Bean Curd, Szechuan Style (with pork)   6.25

Bean Curd, Country Style (with pork)   6.25

Shredded Pork with Hoisin Sauce   6.55

Moo Shu Pork with Pancakes (4)   6.55
(additional pancakes 20¢ each)

Gung Bo Gai Ding   7.75
(Diced chicken meat, blended w/cashews, mushrooms and vegetables in chili sauce)

Gung Bo Beef Ding   8.10

Chef's Suggestions
Per Order

Lung Har Kew   9.95
Breaded fresh lobster meat, sautéed with Chinese black mushrooms, water chestnuts, and fresh vegetables

Lung Har Char Sue   10.45
Pan   Lobster meat and roast pork sautéed with Chinese vegetables

Lung Har Gai Kew   10.55
Breaded chicken chunks, lobster meat sautéed with fresh mixed Chinese vegetables

Chow Hoy Sien   11.95
Fresh lobster meat, shrimp & shrimp ball with fresh Chinese vegetables

Shrimp Balls   Shrimp   9.55
balls sautéed with Chinese vegetables, snow peas, bamboo shoots, water chestnuts and mushrooms

Har Kew Char Sue   9.55
Pan   Breaded fresh jumbo shrimp and roast pork, sautéed with mushrooms, bamboo shoots, water chestnuts, snow pea pods and bok toy

Chow Gai Kew   6.95
Breaded boneless chicken sautéed with mixed Chinese vegetables

Shoot Dow Gai Kew   7.40
Fresh boneless chicken sautéed with black mushrooms, snow pea pods, and vegetables

Subgum Mor Good   7.55
Gai   Fried boneless chicken, subgum vegetables & mushroom sauce and garnished with sliced Virginia ham, roast pork, and white meat chicken

Phoenix Chicken   7.75
Fried boneless breast of chicken meat with Virginia ham over a bed of assorted vegetables

Li Chee Opp   Slightly   6.90
braised boneless duckling, li chee fruit with sweet and pungent sauce

Moo Goo Ho Yu Ngow   5.95
Tender beef with mushroom and oyster sauce

Chow Steak Kew   12.50
Cube filet of beef sautéed with snow pea pods, bamboo shoots, water chestnuts and fresh vegetables

Som God Tai   Sliced   9.95
white meat chicken, roast pork and lobster meat sautéed with snow pea pods, bamboo shoots, water chestnuts and bok toy

Subgum Wonton   9.95
Fried wonton, sliced chicken, lobster meat, roast pork, black mushrooms and mixed Chinese vegetables

Cookies

1 Doz.   1.10   ½ Doz.   .65

Noodles

Lg.   .65   Small   .50

Chinese Restaurant

Not only are Chinese restaurants becoming increasingly popular, but they're good places to find a Pritikin meal—from wonton soup to lichee nuts. You'll have to skip some of the courses in between, however, like the fried appetizers, including such items as egg rolls, featured on this fairly typical Chinese menu (pages 104–106). Note that the menu shown is designed for takeout orders, but similar fare is offered in restaurants where you dine on-premises. The appetizer section on Chinese menus—where you usually find egg rolls—is rarely promising for Pritikinites. On this menu, steamed dim sum could be all right, especially with a vegetable or seafood filling, but these dishes may be made with egg noodle dough and pork. You can ask about the dim sum in the particular Chinese restaurant where you're dining. Barbecued ribs are, of course, too high in fat.

The soup section generally offers better prospects, though soups vary from restaurant to restaurant as to how salty or oily they are. With luck, the Chinese restaurant you visit will use a chicken broth base that is practically fat-free and very lightly salted. Ask. On this menu, the wonton soup could be acceptable. Don't order the egg-drop soup or other dishes containing egg yolk such as the egg foo young. Noodles usually contain egg yolk, too, and are often fried, so it's best to avoid them. (On this menu, noodle dishes appear under "Chow Mein" and "Lo Mein.")

When choosing your Chinese dish, select one with lots of vegetables and a small amount of chicken, meat, or shellfish, remembering that shrimp is especially high in cholesterol, so you should have only half the usual portion. Pork is a high-fat meat, so the amount of pork used should be very small if you choose a pork-and-vegetable dish. Cantonese-style dishes generally use meat, poultry, or shellfish more as a taste enhancer than as the main ingredient in a dish. Not only are Szechuan, Mandarin, and Hunan cuisines spicier, but most of the dishes contain more oil and meat. You can, however, request that stock be used in the wok instead of oil, or that oil be kept to a bare minimum.

Many Chinese restaurants have a vegetable or vegetarian section, although this one doesn't. Sai Wu does, however, offer a vegetable chop suey (under "Chop Suey") and could undoubtedly fix other kinds of vegetable dishes for you upon request. Vegetable dishes will usually feature broccoli, Chinese cabbage, snow peas, bamboo shoots, bean sprouts, water chestnuts, tomatoes, bell peppers, and an assortment of Chinese mushrooms.

In Chinese restaurants, it's best to order *à la carte*. Dinners invariably include deep-fried items, as well as fried rice and often fried noodles. Ask to have your dishes cooked in broth or water, or in a bare minimum of oil. And to accompany your meal, order plenty of plain steamed rice (a good complex-carbohydrate food, although unfortunately deprived of some of the nutrients you get at home with your brown rice).

The following selections are some of the good choices from this menu: under "Poultry"—moo goo gai pan (white meat chicken, mushrooms, water chestnuts, bamboo shoots, and vegetables) and bo lo gai pan (white meat chicken, pineapple, and Chinese vegetables); under "Sea Food"—lobster Cantonese-style; and under "Chop Suey"—vegetable chop suey, an especially good choice if you are ordering other dishes containing meat, shellfish, or poultry and wish to have another dish to round out your meal.

For an additional discussion on ordering food in Chinese restaurants, (including information about bean curd, often featured prominently on Chinese menus, although not on this one), see pages 60–61.

Salta in Bocca

179 Madison Avenue
New York, NY 10016
(212) 882-5243

Antipasti
Appetizers

Antipasti Variati 4.00
 Mixed Cold Appetizers
Prosciutto e Melone 4.00
Peperoni al Forno con 4.00
 Alici Roasted Fresh
 Peppers with Anchovies
Vongole nel Guscio 4.00
 Clams on the Half Shell
Sedani e Olive Celery 3.00
 and Olives
Spiedino Romana 4.50
 Bread Skewer Mozzarella
 and Ham in a Capers and
 Anchovies Sauce

Vongole e Muscoli al 4.50
 Vino Bianco Clams
 and Mussels Steamed in
 White Wine
Scampi Saltati 6.00
 Shrimps Sautéed
Vongole Oreganate o 4.50
 Casino Baked Clams
Muscoli Della Riviera 3.50
 Mussels Steamed in Red
 Sauce
Zuppa di Vongole 4.50
 Clams Steamed in White
 Wine and Shallots
Antipasto Salta Baked 6.00
 Clams, Shrimps and
 Mussels in Red Sauce

Minestre
Soups

Minestrone Fresh 3.00
 Vegetable Soup
Pasta e Fagioli Beans 3.00
 and Pasta
Zuppa di Spinaci 3.00
 Spinach Soup

Stracciatella Eggdrop 3.00
 Soup with Spinach
Cappelletti in Brodo 3.00
 Meat Dumplings in Broth
Pastina in Brodo 3.00
 Consommé with Pastina

Farinacei
Farinaceous

Fettuccine Romana 11.00
 Egg Noodles in White
 Cream Sauce
Trenette al Pesto 12.00
 Thin Egg Noodles in Green
 Basil Sauce
Lasagna Salta Home- 11.00
 made Baked Lasagna
Cannelloni di Carne 11.00
 Meat Cannelloni
Manicotti di Ricotta 11.00
 Ricotta Cheese Manicotti

Fettuccine Casalinga 11.00
 White and Green Noodles
 in White Cream Sauce with
 Prosciutto, Onions, and Peas
Spaghetti Carbonara 11.00
 Spaghetti with Onions, Pros-
 ciutto, Cheese and Egg Yolk
Spaghetti al Sugo 11.00
 Spaghetti with Meat Sauce
Taglierini Marinara 11.00
 Thin Egg Noodles in Mari-
 nara Sauce

109

Capelli D'Angelo   11.00
Angel's Hair

Linguine alle Vongole 11.00
Linguine in White or Red
Clam Sauce

Paglia e Fieno   Thin   11.00
White and Green Noodles in
a White Cream Sauce with
Prosciutto and Peas

Tortellini Gratinati   11.00
Meat Dumplings Au Gratin

Combinazione   11.00
Manicotti-Cannelloni

Fettuccine Verdi   11.00
Amatriciana   Green
Noodles in Fresh Filet of
Tomato Sauce with
Prosciutto and Onions

Spaghetti al Filetto   11.00
Spaghetti in a Fresh Filet of
Tomato Sauce

Pesci
Fish

Sogliola alle   14.00
Mandorle   Filet of Sole
"Amandine"

Spigola Piccante   14.00
Striped Bass in Wine, Capers
and Anchovies

Sogliola Nostrana   14.00
Mugnaia   Filet of Sole
Sautéed "Meuniere"

Scampi al Vino   16.00
Bianco   Shrimps
Sautéed in White Wine

Cernia Livornese   16.00
Red Snapper in Red Sauce
with Green and Black
Olives, Onions, and Capers

Cernia alla Griglia   15.00
Broiled Red Snapper

Calamaretti Fritti   14.00
Fried Squid

Scampi fra Diavolo   16.00
Shrimps Sautéed in a Spicy
Tomato Sauce

Vongole o Cozze   12.00
Veneziana   Clams or Mussels Steamed in White Wine

Calamari Barcaiola   14.00
Squid in White Wine Sauce
with Shallots & Tomato

Spigola Bollita   13.00
Poached Striped Bass

Spigola Triestina   15.00
Striped Bass Sautéed in White
Wine Sauce with Mussels and
Clams

Carni
Meats

Pollo Parmigiana   12.00
Chicken Parmigiana

Pollo a la Romana   12.00
Boneless Chicken in Wine
Sauce with Artichokes &
Mushrooms

Pollo Francese   12.00
Boneless Breast of
Chicken in White Wine

Pollo Cacciatora   12.00
Boneless Chicken in Tomato
and Mushroom Sauce

Pollo Scarpara   12.00
Boneless Chicken Battered
in Garlic and Shallots

Pollo Piccata   12.00
Boneless Breast of Chicken
in Butter and Lemon Sauce

Fegatini di Pollo   12.00
Veneta   Chicken Livers in
White Wine and Onion Sauce

Bistecca di Manzo   16.00
Sirloin Steak

Medaglioni di Bue   16.00
Mignonettes of Beef

Salsiccia Friulana   13.00
Sausage in Marinara Sauce
with Peppers and Mushrooms

Vitello Genovese   Veal 15.00
in a Green Basil Sauce

Vitello Paillard	16.00	**Vitello Bolognese**	14.00
Veal Paillard		Veal with Prosciutto and	
Costoletta Bolognese	16.00	Mozzarella Cheese	
Butterflied Veal Chop with		**Vitello alla Francese**	14.00
Prosciutto and Cheese		Veal in a Light White Wine	
Costoletta di Vitello	16.00	Sauce	
Milanese Breaded Veal		**Vitello Boscaiola**	14.00
Cutlet		Veal, Red Wine Sauce with	
Vitello Parmigiana	14.00	Peas, Onions and	
Veal Parmigiana		Mushrooms	
Costoletta alla	15.00	**Fegato di Vitello**	15.00
Fiorentina Veal Cutlet		**Veneziana** Calf's Liver in	
Stuffed with Ricotta Cheese,		White Wine and Onion Sauce	
Prosciutto & Spinach		**Scaloppine Salta in**	15.00
Vitello Pizzaiola	14.00	**Bocca** Veal with Spinach,	
Veal in Marinara Sauce with		Prosciutto and Sage	
Mushrooms and Peppers		**Costoletta di Vitello**	18.00
Scaloppine Marsala	14.00	**alla Griglia** Grilled	
Veal in Marsala Wine and		Veal Chop	
Mushroom Sauce			

Legumi
Vegetables

Zucchini Fritti Fried	3.50	**Funghi Trifolati**	3.00
Zucchini		Mushrooms Sautéed	
Spinaci al Burro	3.00	**Fagiolini Marinara**	3.00
Spinach Sautéed in Butter		String Beans Sautéed	
Piselli al Prosciutto	3.00	Marinara	
Peas Sautéed with Prosciutto		**Melanzane**	9.00
		Parmigiana Eggplant	
		Parmigiana	

Insalata
Salads

Insalata Mista Mixed	3.00	**Insalata Primavera**	3.50
Green Salad		Special House Salad	
Romana Romaine	3.00	**Fagiolini e**	3.50
Lettuce		**Barbabietole** String	
Lattuga e Pomodoro	3.00	Beans & Beetroot	
Lettuce and Tomato		**Indivia Belga** Endive	4.00
Rugola Arrugula	4.00	Lettuce	
Insalata di Spinaci e	4.50	**Insalata di Pomodori**	3.00
Funghi Raw Spinach and		Sliced Tomato	
Mushrooms Salad		**Insalata Cesare**	9.00
		Caesar Salad for Two	

111

Dolci e Gelati
Desserts

Zuppa Inglese Rum Cake	3.00	**Fragole Fresche** Fresh 3.50 Strawberries
Torta di Formaggio Cheese Cake	3.00	**Fragole alla Salta** 4.50 Strawberries Special
Torta della Casa	4.00	**Melone di Stagione** 3.00
Tartufo all Salta	5.00	Melon in Season
Gelati Vari Ice Cream, Assorted Flavors	2.50	**Sorbetti** Sherbets 2.50
Zabaione	4.00	**Spumoni e Tortoni** 2.00

Caffe

Espresso	1.50	Te	1.00
Caffe	1.00	Cappuccino	2.00
Sanka	1.00	Caffe Salta	4.00

Italian Restaurant

Most Italian restaurants offer a range of entrées, but their main emphasis is on pasta dishes and pizzas. More elegant restaurants such as Salta in Bocca, which features Northern Italian fare, offer an assortment of fish, veal, chicken, beef, and vegetable as well as pasta dishes. Salta in Bocca's menu (pages 109–112) is fairly typical of fine Italian restaurants. Let's suppose you were dining there.

There are several enticing prospects among the soups ("Minestre") and salads ("Insalata"). Good soup choices might be the minestrone (fresh vegetable soup) and the pasta e fagioli (beans and pasta). The pastina in brodo (consommé with pastina) could be a good choice, but the pastina might be made with egg yolk. Better Italian restaurants frequently feature many kinds of pasta that are made with egg yolk, so before you order any dish, make sure that the pasta it contains was not made with this super cholesterol-rich ingredient. Also ask whether the soups contain much fat. In better-quality restaurants, you are not likely to have this problem, but it's best to inquire.

Except for the Caesar salad, which is contaminated with cheese, oil, and egg yolk, there is a wonderful array of salads to choose from. The salad with spinach (as well as the spinach soup) would be all right occasionally, but spinach (as explained on page 94) is not a preferred vegetable. Any of the salads would be delicious with a little chopped fresh basil (or other fresh herb) and lemon juice or wine vinegar, mixed with a little crushed fresh garlic if possible.

Among the pastas ("Farinacei"), a glance at the menu tells you to bypass most of the dishes because they contain (1) egg noodles or egg yolk; (2) cream sauce; or (3) cheese. The clue to a cheese entrée may appear in the name—as in tortellini gratinati (meat dumplings au gratin) or manicotti di ricotta (ricotta cheese manicotti)—but sometimes the name is no help. In the latter case, it is necessary to be familiar with Italian dishes or to ask your waiter. Lasagna and cannelloni are two cheese-filled dishes to be avoided.

The pasta dishes that you could consider are spaghetti al sugo (spaghetti with meat sauce), linguine alle vongole (linguine in clam sauce—choose the red), and spaghetti al filetto (spaghetti in a fresh filet of tomato sauce). But before you place an order, be sure to find out about the sauce. Does it contain butter or oil? If so, can the sauce be made without this ingredient? If you are reassured on that count and the pasta used does not contain egg yolk, go ahead—but remind your waiter to tell the chef not to pour oil or melted butter on the noodles and not to sprinkle Parmesan cheese over the top.

You could ask for half an order of the vegetarian spaghetti (spaghetti al filetto) and split an order of fish or chicken with a dining partner. Skip the veal dishes. Veal has an undeserved reputation as a low-fat meat. It's actually higher in both fat and cholesterol than lean beef (such as round or flank steak). Naturally, you'll pass on the sirloin steak, sausage, and liver entrées for similar reasons.

Under the fish selections ("Pesci"), the calamari (squid) is a good choice—if you like it—because it is especially low in both fat and cholesterol. But don't choose the fried squid. Ask for any of the fish entrées broiled dry or with a little lemon juice, or poached in wine sauce. Shrimp is a high-cholesterol item, so if you choose the shrimp dish, your portion size should be reduced to half the 3½-ounce-per-day total allotment for animal foods. Clams, however, are a low-cholesterol shellfish, subject to the regular portion limits.

Among the meat selections, the boneless breast of chicken in white wine (pollo Francese) looks like your best bet. If you want a vegetable, see whether you can have it sautéed in a little wine and broth, or steamed. Typical of fine Italian restaurants, this one offers fresh fruit for dessert. If fruit isn't listed on the menu, you should ask; fruit is usually available.

For an additional discussion of how to order in Italian restaurants, see pages 62–63.

Wendy's®

Sandwich Choices

¼ lb.* Single Hamburger	$1.19	¾ lb.* Triple Hamburger	$2.39
w/cheese	1.34	w/cheese	2.54
½ lb.* Double Hamburger	1.95	Chicken Breast Filet	1.85
w/cheese	2.10	w/cheese	2.00

Net weight before cooking

Condiment Choices

Mayonnaise, ketchup, pickle, onion, lettuce, mustard.
Tomato .10 extra

Kid's Fun Pack $1.49

Includes Junior Hamburger, Junior Fries, Junior
Soft Drink and a Junior Frosty. Also a special surprise!

Salad $2.25

All you can eat! Includes your choice of dressings:
Blue Cheese, French, Thousand Island, Italian, Lo-Cal Italian or
our House Dressing

Taco Salad $2.25

Taco Chips, Lettuce, Tomato and Cheese smothered in
Wendy's famous Chili.
Sour Cream-flavored topping .20 extra.

French Fries .65

Chili—Large: $1.45   Regular: $1.09   Cheese: .15
Frosty—Large: $1.09   Medium: .95   Small: .75
Dairy Dessert, available in light chocolate.

Soft Drinks

Small: .50   Medium: .60   Large: .70
Pepsi, Diet Pepsi, Dr. Pepper, Root Beer,
Mountain Dew, Lemonade, Fruit Punch

Iced Tea—Large: .70   Regular: .60
Coffee—.35   Milk—.45

Fast-Food Restaurant

In the past 25 years, the term "fast food" has become common in the English language, and eating in fast-food restaurants has become an integral part of life for masses of Americans.

In other cultures, fast foods are ancient and universal. Street vendors selling various snacks and light meals were popular in Roman times. Handmade fast foods are found all over the world—tacos in Mexico, chapatis (unleavened bread) and curry in India, pita bread stuffed with minced mutton in the eastern Mediterranean, or Chinese quick wok or noodle dishes.

In the West, fast foods differ from such traditionally sold items in that national chains (sometimes international) have been formed to provide highly advertised meals produced for mass distribution and consumption. These food items are generally compact, cooked meals or near-meals that can be eaten on the spot or prepared "to go." The fast-food chains include hamburger and fried-chicken operations, pizza parlors, and steak houses. Augmenting these are other fast-food-type operations, such as individually-owned sandwich shops and delicatessens.

Whether or not we view the phenomenal growth of fast-food restaurants as regrettable, these restaurants have obvious appeal to Americans, who purchase about 25% of their meals eaten outside the home in restaurants of this type. Consumers are attracted to the quick service, convenience, and reasonable prices, which they know about only too well, thanks to the millions of dollars spent on television and other forms of advertising to beguile the public.

The terms "fast food" and "junk food" are synonymous in the minds of many. But, in fact, fast-food restaurants are often not much worse than or different from many standard restaurants in offering food that is excessively high in calories, fat, cholesterol, sugar, and salt, and low in vitamins, minerals, and fiber. Besides, with the recent trend toward incorporating salad-bar operations into the food service of fast-food restaurants, an occasional salad meal at such an establishment may be satisfactory from the Pritikin dieter's standpoint, as would be the case with Wendy's, the fast-food restaurant whose menu appears on page 115. (The menu is that offered in Wendy's branches in Santa Barbara, California.) Not yet shown on the menu is the baked potato, a new feature item now offered by Wendy's restaurants across the nation.

If you find it convenient or otherwise desirable to eat at a fast-food restaurant from time to time, be armed with the following guidelines and information to help you select healthful meals without compromising your dietary commitments. First, select a fast-food restaurant that offers a salad bar and—if possible—baked potatoes. Chemicals such as sulfites are sometimes added to salads to preserve freshness, and you would want to avoid that. We have been assured by the following national fast-food chains that their produce has not been so treated, but you should check at the particular fast-food restaurant that you frequent.

ARBY'S. Offers a salad bar. Available in most states.

BONANZA. Offers a salad bar and baked potatoes.

BURGER KING. Offers a salad bar and salad served in a pita.

MARRIOTT HOTELS. Serves salads, entrées, and breakfasts that are low in fat and cholesterol.

PIZZA HUT. Offers a salad bar.

SIZZLER STEAKHOUSE. Offers a salad bar and baked potatoes.

SKINNY HAVEN. Offers various vegetable and chicken dishes.

WENDY'S. Offers a salad bar and baked potatoes.

In restaurants that serve baked potatoes, none of the usual toppings are acceptable, but you could add some chopped scallions or other vegetables from the bar. One of the fast-food chains, Burger King, offers pita bread, so customers can make salad-stuffed pita-bread sandwiches, which could be a nice change from baked potatoes.

Next, avoid items at the salad bar that are mixed with dressings, such as potato, carrot, and macaroni salads, which contain mayonnaise or oil. Most salad dressings provided will not be acceptable for the same reason. Dress your salad, instead, with a little vinegar or a squeeze of lemon. Or do as some do, and take your own dressing* with you in a small, tightly closed container.

Salad bars at more expensive restaurants may have fresh fruits, but at a fast-food operation, you are likely to encounter canned fruits in heavy sugar syrups, which should be avoided.

---

*Recipes for salad dressings can be found in other books about the Pritikin Program. (See page 135 for a list of these books.)

Fast-food staples—hamburgers, cheeseburgers, hot dogs, pizza, French fries, and most other meal choices—are laden with fat and cholesterol. Fatty meats, high-fat cheeses, and deep-fat frying are the culprits in most cases. Even the chicken-breast filet on the Wendy's menu is fried in deep fat. Any of these foods would be inappropriate for Pritikin diners.

Typical fast-food meals are very high in salt as well. Lavish use of high-salt condiments, such as ketchup, pickles, mustard, mayonnaise, and salad dressings, are major offenders here. (A fast-food meal often contains as much as 2,500 mg of sodium—almost as much as the sodium intake for the average American for the entire day.) Your general rule ought to be to avoid the fat- or oil-containing condiments, such as mayonnaise or the usual salad dressings, and to restrict the use of condiments that are free of fat or oil but are still high in salt, such as pickles and mustard. Help yourself to a *small* amount of these or avoid them also.

If you are ordering in a delicatessen or sandwich shop, select acceptable breads such as pita (preferably whole-wheat), sourdough, French, pumpernickel, and rye—favoring the kinds without added fat, oil, or sugar. In some establishments, you'll find whole-wheat or water bagels too.

Ask for sliced fresh tomatoes, lettuce, onions, cucumber, or sprouts to create a vegetarian sandwich or to accompany meat choices. Watch your portion size when you choose meat items, and favor meats like turkey or chicken breast. Roast beef, unless unusually lean, will generally be substantially higher in fat content. Water-packed tuna would be another good choice. Your portion should not exceed 3½ ounces, since your total daily allotment for meat, poultry, or seafood is that amount.

Beverages in a fast-food restaurant are likely to feature milkshakes or similar high-fat dairy concoctions, such as Wendy's frosty, and soft drinks, those abominations created by infusing perfectly good water with large amounts of sugar, artificial flavorings, and numerous chemical additives. As in any restaurant, your best beverage bet is hot water with lemon, or bring your own chamomile or red-bush herb tea bag. Several steak houses have been offering nonfat milk as an à la carte item, which could be another beverage choice for you.

Like it or not, fast-food restaurants are a way of life in America—and even in many parts of the world. What traveler has not been appalled by the sight of a McDonald's in foreign cities, sometimes near some treasured relic? Cultural and historical considerations aside, this need not be something to deplore, if you can find a good salad bar in this fast-food outpost!

Zachariah's

Golden Nugget Hotel
First and Fremont Streets
Las Vegas, Nevada 89101
(702) 385-7111

For Good Health . . . and Good Eating . . . the Golden Nugget Presents
THE PRITIKIN MENU

A permanent and pleasant way of dining that may add glowing, vibrant years to your life. Every delicious dish is prepared without salt, sugar or fat, according to the precepts of one of the world's most famous health experts, Nathan Pritikin.

Breakfast All Day

Omelet *with Hoop and Sapsago Cheeses Toast, Baked Hash Browns*	4.75
Apple and Oats Cereal	3.55
Pritikin Muffin *with Diet Jam*	1.95

Appetizers

Mushrooms with Vegetable Stuffing and Sapsago Cheese	3.25
Jicama Spears and Red Apples	3.25

Soups

Vegetable—Chicken Rice Creole—Barley
Cup 1.95   Bowl 2.55

Refreshing Salads

Fresh Fruit Plate *with Special Fruit Dressing*	5.55
Creole Jambalaya *with Breast of Chicken*	5.25
Pineapple Chicken Salad	5.25
Marinated Bean Sprouts and Mushrooms *with Cucumbers and Peppers*	4.95

Entrées
Served with Brown Rice and Vegetables

Breast of Chicken, *Malaysian Style*	9.25
Baked Cod Creole *with Tomatoes, Bell Peppers and Onions*	9.25
Fresh Turkey Breast Cacciatore	9.25

Desserts

Homemade Pritikin Puddings	1.75
Banana Rice, Tapioca, Apple Pudding Cake	
Frozen Banana with Skim Milk	1.95

Beverages

Natural Apple Juice or Natural Grape Juice	1.50
Fresh Orange Juice	1.75
Nonfat Milk 1.00 Hot Chamomile Tea 1.00	

119

A Special Pritikin Menu*

The Golden Nugget in Las Vegas has a special Pritikin menu* (page 119). While not particularly extensive, it covers all the basics plus gourmet delicacies such as muffins, omelets, puddings, and several interesting salads and hot entrées.

The restaurant's menu has other sections too (not reproduced here) that feature "regular" food. For Pritikinites, the pickings from these pages of the menu would be slim, but from them you could order a breast of turkey sandwich, a toasted bagel, or, if you've hit the jackpot and are ready to splurge, broiled lobster tail, without the melted butter.

---

*The name "Pritikin" is used by arrangement with Pritikin Programs, P.O. Box 5335, Santa Barbara, CA 93108.

7

Suggestions for Your Restaurateur

Wouldn't it be "loverly"—as Eliza Doolittle said—if *more* restaurants offered Pritikin-type foods to patrons desiring it? Or if restaurants currently accommodating Pritikin dieters with a few foods expanded the number of choices available to them?

Perhaps you know a restaurateur or two who would like to do this but who need a little help getting started. If you do, you might share some of the material in this section with them.

General instructions are provided here that could be utilized by any type of restaurant interested in appealing to Pritikin diners. Even putting a very few items into a standard menu would be helpful; but ambitious restaurateurs might want to create more complete menus, choosing from the suggestions that follow, items most in keeping with the general format of their restaurants.

An example of a basic but very adequate Pritikin-type menu is the one on page 122 offered by Chancellor's,* a restaurant in Houston, Texas. The menu is suitable for either lunch or dinner, and items include a basic pita sandwich, vegetable stew (ratatouille), baked potatoes, hot and cold soups, several hot entrées and cold salads, and fresh fruit dessert. Chancellor's also offers non-Pritikin fare, such as filet mignon, chicken cordon bleu, broccoli or cauliflower with cheese sauce, and a variety of rich dessert items.

---

*The Pritikin name is not used on the menu, but the menu items follow Pritikin guidelines or are based on recipes published in earlier books on the Pritikin Program. Special arrangements with Pritikin Programs would be required to permit use of the name "Pritikin" on any restaurant menu.

Chancellor's

6535 Dumfries
Houston, Texas 77096
(713) 772-9955

Help Your Heart
NO SALT, NO SUGAR, LOW FAT

Soups

Gazpacho	Cup	*$1.65*	*Broccoli Bisque*	Cup	*$1.65*
	Bowl	*$2.50*		Bowl	*$2.50*

Salads

Tabouli   *A tasty mixture of bulghur wheat, fresh mint,*   **$3.25**
parsley, and vegetables. Served with whole wheat pita.

Mixed green   *Fresh greens with mushrooms,*   Small   **$1.50**
green onion, and cherry tomatoes.   Large   **$3.50**

Salad Bar   *With special dressing.*   **$6.25**

Entrées

Fresh Fish of the Day   Priced Daily

Steamed Chicken Breast   *Served plain or with a light*   **$8.95**
tomato sauce or an apple glaze.

Pita Sandwich   *A crunchy mix of fresh raw vegetables*   **$6.95**
with steamed chicken or tuna. Served with a special
dressing.

Chicken Stir-Fry   *A colorful assortment of fresh*   **$8.95**
steamed vegetables and chicken over a bed of rice.
Served with a delicious mild soy sauce.

Chicken Vegetable Paella   *Tender chunks of chicken*   **$9.25**
and brown rice simmered with a tempting blend of
vegetables. Served with ratatouille.

Steamed Vegetable Plate   *A variety of garden fresh*   **$5.95**
vegetables steamed to perfection.

Side Dishes

Ratatouille   *A wonderful blend of Italian vegetables in*   **$3.15**
a light tomato sauce.

Steamed Carrots   *A' la apple.*   **$2.25**

Baked Potato   **$1.50**

Fresh Fruit Dessert   *A chef's assortment of fresh fruits.*   **$2.95**

Suggest to your restaurateurs that they peruse the suggestions in this chapter, with the idea of selecting from various categories (salads, sandwiches, entrées, etc.) those items that could make a nice addition to their restaurant menus. Some of the suggestions for menu items are popular dishes requiring only minor modifications to make them Pritikin-OK, as noted. For convenience, their usual names are retained in the listing, although they have been modified to meet Pritikin guidelines. In other instances, suggested items are dishes that can be prepared by a competent chef by simply following the general instructions provided here.

Frequently, however, a restaurateur will be helped by having access to particular Pritikin recipes; for this purpose, the recipe names appear in italics in the discussions, and on pages 135–140, all recipes mentioned are listed alphabetically, with information on where they appear in earlier Pritikin books. When the recipe has not been published, the reader is instructed to write us for a copy.

No doubt, the suggestions in this section will inspire talented chefs to create their own versions of Pritikin-style dishes, or to improve upon our recipes. We are delighted by this prospect. But before interested restaurateurs embark on creative efforts of their own, we urge them to acquaint themselves thoroughly with the guidelines of the Pritikin Program by studying the "Table of Foods to Use and to Avoid" (pages 10–14) and other material in Chapter 1.

Salads

When Pritikin diners choose a salad, because of the limited possibilities at present, they usually select either a mixed green or a dinner salad or a fresh fruit plate. Wouldn't it be great if there were more interesting possibilities? Here are some suggestions.

Accompany all salads with a choice of rolls or bread, if desired, selecting from Pritikin whole-wheat or rye bread (or equivalents) or sourdough varieties.

Offer suitable oil-free dressings, when appropriate. Good choices are *French Dressing,** *Vinaigrette Dressing, Zesty Tomato Dressing,* and *Cucumber-Yogurt Dressing.*

Chef's Salad

From a regular chef's salad, omit the ham, cheese, and hard-boiled egg yolks. Make a Pritikin-version Chef's Salad by

---

*All recipe names in italics are Pritikin recipes that appear in other Pritikin Program books. See page 135 for information on how to locate these recipes.

substituting strips of turkey breast and chopped egg whites. Add cooked (or canned) kidney or garbanzo beans, canned water-packed artichoke hearts, and cooked or canned cut green beans, asparagus spears, and sliced red beets. Raw vegetable ingredients could include assorted greens (two or more kinds of lettuce, preferably dark green, such as romaine, butterhead, and red leaf, with a little iceberg used for color); shredded red cabbage; grated carrots; chopped celery; sliced radishes, cucumbers, and red onions; chopped scallions, chives, and/or fresh parsley; cherry tomatoes or tomato wedges; and alfalfa or mung bean sprouts.

A nice garnish would be a topping of croutons made from leftover Pritikin whole-wheat or rye bread (or equivalent breads). Make the croutons by oven-toasting cubes of bread and sprinkling them with onion and garlic powders.

Salade Niçoise and Seafarer's Salad

To make a Salade Niçoise, follow directions for the chef's salad, but eliminate the turkey and substitute flaked canned water-packed tuna that has been seasoned with a little dill weed and lemon juice. Other ingredients could include chopped onion, sliced water chestnuts, cauliflower flowerets, and a few capers. To make a Seafarer's Salad, follow the directions for Salade Niçoise, but substitute chunks of cooked lobster or scallops for the tuna.

Pasta Salad

Use flat whole-wheat noodles (linguine) to make *Tuna-Linguine Salad.* Or for a vegetarian version—*Linguine Salad*—omit the tuna. Besides the pasta, and the tuna, if used, the main ingredients are canned water-packed artichokes, frozen green peas, red bell pepper or pimiento, green onion, and seasonings.

Greek Salad

No feta cheese or olives are permitted in our *Greek Salad* (both are too high in fat), but this dish still has quite a bit of the original flavors, since it's made with tomatoes, cucumbers, bell peppers, and red onion, seasoned with oregano, mint, and good vinegars, and sprinkled with crumbly skim-milk cottage cheese.

Creamy Fruit Salad

Creamy Fruit Salad is a very free adaptation of a Waldorf salad, since it has not only apples, celery, and dates, but also bananas, pineapple (canned in its own juice), oranges, grapes, papaya (when available), and jicama or canned water chestnuts. The dressing is made with lowfat cottage cheese (1% fat by weight maximum), nonfat yogurt,* and various seasonings. Serve the salad on a bed of lettuce.

Assorted Fruit Plate

Use seasonal fresh fruits (supplementing them with fruits canned in water or their own juices, if necessary) and oranges, apples, bananas, and so forth. Serve with a side of the dressing used for *Creamy Fruit Salad.*

Tabbouli Salad

Except for the fact that we use no oil, our *Tabbouli Salad,* a Middle Eastern dish, is authentic. The grain required is bulghur wheat, which cooks in stock in 15 minutes. Toss the grain with cut-up scallions, celery, tomato, raw mushrooms, and various seasonings, and serve on lettuce leaves.

Chicken Salad

Make a delicious *Chicken Salad* with cut-up cooked breast of chicken, canned water chestnuts, chopped celery and onion, and seedless grapes. The dressing ingredients include low-fat cottage cheese (1% fat by weight maximum), nonfat yogurt, hard-cooked egg whites, and various seasonings. Since the amount of chicken used needs to be restricted to meet Pritikin guidelines, you may wish to fill out the plate by serving the salad stuffed in a tomato or a cantaloupe half. Place on a bed of lettuce and surround with sliced tomatoes, chilled cooked asparagus spears, and other vegetables.

Sandwiches

A wide variety of interesting, acceptable sandwiches can be created. These can be accompanied by Pritikin-style *Cole Slaw, Potato Salad,* or *"French Fries."* Two long-keeping pickled items would be good for sandwich-making: use *Pickle Relish* as an ingredient in some sandwich fillings, and garnish sandwiches with *Pickled Cucumbers.*

Select good breads for sandwiches. Pritikin breads (available in many stores) make wonderful toast, so choose whole-wheat or rye types or Pritikin English muffins (or find equivalent-quality breads). Whole-wheat pita, chapatis, and bagels are especially appropriate for some sandwiches.

---

*Nonfat yogurt is available in stores in some areas, or send for our recipe: Pritikin Programs, P.O. Box 5335, Santa Barbara, CA 93108.

Sliced Breast of Turkey or Chicken Sandwich

Place thin slices of turkey or chicken on bread of choice. Spread with *Mustard-Yogurt Topping* (made with nonfat yogurt and Dijon mustard—low-salt variety preferred), and serve the sandwich with lettuce leaves and tomato and cucumber slices.

Tuna Salad Sandwich

Our *Tuna Salad* is made with canned water-packed tuna, canned chili salsa, chopped onion and celery, and hard-boiled egg whites. The salad is dressed with a mixture of prepared mustard and nonfat yogurt, seasoned with dill weed and other ingredients. Spread a thin layer of the tuna salad on the bread, and pile on lettuce leaves, sliced tomatoes, thin slices of cucumber, and alfalfa sprouts.

Cheese-Based Pâté Sandwiches

Choose *Salmon Pâté, Egg-Cheese Pâté,* or *Pimiento Cheese* (remarkably like its cream-cheese–based original). All are made with a cottage-cheese base (1% fat by weight maximum) and keep well when refrigerated. *Salmon Pâté* is made by blending several canned ingredients (pink salmon, pimientos, and water-packed artichokes) and seasonings into the cheese base. *Egg-Cheese Pâté* is made by blending hard-cooked egg whites and seasonings into the cheese base. Besides using *Egg-Cheese Pâté* as a spread, try it for making mock deviled eggs, mounding the pâté into the cavity of a hard-cooked egg-white half.

Serve any of the pâtés on a toasted whole-wheat bagel, Pritikin English muffin, or other suitable bread, accompanied by lettuce leaves, tomato and cucumber slices, and alfalfa sprouts.

Cheese-Based Fruit Sandwiches

Blend a little nonfat milk and canned unsweetened apple juice into cottage cheese (1% fat by weight maximum) to make a smooth mixture, and top with your choice of sliced fresh fruits—banana, nectarine, peach, or pear. Lettuce leaves or alfalfa sprouts are optional additions to the sandwich (yes, it will taste good!).

Cooked fruits may also be used over a base of the cheese spread, or they may be used as a spread by themselves. Try the delicious *Cranberry-Apple Compote* on toast or muffins as a jam or as a topping for a cheese layer. This compote, which is thickened with pectin, can also be made with other fruits.

Raw-Vegetable Sandwiches

Just raw vegetables can make delicious sandwiches. Pita bread, into which they can be stuffed, often works best, but sometimes other breads seem more suitable. Use a dressing to add interest, such as *Mustard-Yogurt Topping*.

Try a sandwich of grated carrots, sliced onion and tomato, lettuce leaves, and sprouts, tucking in a few *Pickled Cucumbers*.

Or try thinly sliced red onions, sliced tomatoes, and sliced pepperoncinis, adding lettuce, sprouts, and *Mustard-Yogurt Topping*.

If you want, you can create a mock "lox-and-bagel" sandwich. Instead of the *Mustard-Yogurt Topping*, spread a layer of *Salmon Pâté* on a bagel and top it with raw vegetables such as onion and tomato slices and sprouts.

You can vary raw-vegetable sandwiches with such ingredients as a little flaked tuna, sliced hard-cooked egg whites, or a layer of mashed cooked red or pinto beans that have been mixed with seasonings and a little nonfat yogurt.

Other Sandwiches

The *Chicken Salad* (without the grapes) would also make a good sandwich. Or consider a sandwich made with our *Breaded Fish*, delicately seasoned and breaded, oven-baked (without oils), and served on Pritikin rye (or other suitable bread) with a special *Fish Dressing*.

Soups

Many of your current soup recipes can be adapted to Pritikin guidelines by simply omitting oils or fats. Vegetables can be sautéed in broth or stock, instead of butter or oil; and meat stocks or chicken stocks, when used as the soup base or to boost flavor, should be thoroughly defatted. Preferably, grains or pasta (never egg pasta) added to soups should be the whole-grain forms. A few suggestions follow.

Legume Soups

Split peas, lentils, lima beans, or other beans (but not soybeans, which are too high in fat), or combinations of beans, can be used to make great Pritikin-style soups, using a vegetable stock or a water base, chopped vegetables, and suitable seasonings. Run a portion of the soup through a blender, then return it to the pot, to give the soup a thicker, more flavorful base. Some fine legume soups are *Hearty Lentil Soup*, *White Bean-and-Turkey Soup*, *Garbanzo Minestrone*, *Split Pea Soup*, *Lentil Soup*, and *Eight-Bean Soup*.

Vegetable Soups

Use a strong vegetable stock for increased flavor. A few soups to consider are *Tomato Bouillon, Tomato-Okra Soup, Chinese Tomato-Vegetable Soup, Tomato-Rice Soup,* and *Vegetable-Barley Soup.*

Chilled Soups

Some recommendations are *Chilled Cucumber Soup, Carrot-Leek Soup, Gazpacho,* and *Beet Borscht.* Serve the chilled soups with a garnish of nonfat yogurt or *Mock Sour Cream.* (The carrot-leek soup and borscht are also good served hot.)

Main-Dish Soups

Heartier soups that make delicious meals by themselves, with the addition of a green salad and lots of good bread, are *Creamy Fish Chowder, Cioppino,* and *Chicken and Okra Gumbo.*

Entrées

The suggestions that follow are for both full-dinner and light-dinner menus. Many of them are also suitable for luncheon menus. A few suggestions with an ethnic slant are also included; these could be used in restaurants serving Chinese, Italian, or Mexican fare, as well as in regular restaurants. Most of the entrées use some form of poultry, seafood, or meat, but a few vegetarian preparations are also discussed.

Portion sizes of poultry, seafood, and meat should not exceed 3½ ounces per serving, and low-fat, low-cholesterol kinds of these foods are preferred, as will be noted. (See also chart on pages 10–14.)

However prepared, these recipes should be served with ample portions of suitable complex-carbohydrate foods—green and yellow vegetables and starches, such as potatoes, whole grains, and whole-wheat pasta. Good starchy choices include plain steamed brown rice or a tasty pilaf, such as our *Herbed Rice Pilaf;* baked potatoes (accompanied by chopped chives and *Mock Sour Cream*) or *Mashed Potatoes;* corn on the cob; and sweet potato or yam, served baked in the shell or mashed with other ingredients for a fancier presentation, as for a holiday dinner with sliced roast turkey breast. You could provide another complex-carbohydrate traditional "fixing" for this holiday meal with a stuffing using *Corn Bread* as the base. Add the usual ingredients, such as chopped celery and onion and seasonings, moisten with defatted chicken or turkey stock, and stir in a few chopped roasted chestnuts.

(Chestnuts are the *only* nut permitted on the Pritikin diet, because they are very low in fat, in sharp contrast to other nuts.)

Chicken Breasts and Turkey Breasts

Chicken breasts and turkey breasts are favored animal foods on the Pritikin diet because the white meat of chicken and turkey is quite low in fat and not excessively high in cholesterol. In addition, both are versatile foods that creative chefs enjoy using.

In the allotted portion size, chicken breast cut into chunks is especially good in casserole or stir-fry dishes. But that amount of chicken is also adequate when the chicken is left uncut and served with an ample portion of rice, pasta, or other starchy food.

Some excellent recipes using chicken breasts are *Chicken Breasts aux Champignons, Stuffed Breast of Chicken with Lemon-Wine Sauce, Jade Empress Chicken, Chicken and Potatoes in Mushroom-Tomato Sauce, Chinese-Sesame Chicken Salad, Sri Lanka Chicken Curry,* and *Oven-Baked Breaded Chicken.*

In the same portion size, turkey breast is also an excellent choice for Pritikin entrées. Slices of uncooked turkey breast lend themselves well to interesting recipes such as *Turkey "Fried" Steak* and *Turkey Breast Slices in Wine-Caper Sauce.* Cooked and cut into chunks, turkey breast can be used in such dishes as *Turkey Tetrazzini.* Or roasted whole and then sliced, turkey breast is perfect for holiday meals. (Use it at other times for sandwiches or salads.)

Fish Filets or Fish Steaks

Fish is just as versatile as white meat chicken or turkey and equally desirable for Pritikin dieters. Control portion size (3½ ounces per serving) and use lean fish and suitable cooking techniques, such as broiling without oil or fats (use lemon juice or other oil-free basting liquids and suitable seasonings), poaching in white wine and/or fish stock, oil-free sautéing (use a small quantity of poaching liquids), or baking. Some excellent recipes for baking or steaming fish using breading or sauces are *Oven-Baked Breaded Filet of Sole* served with *Spicy Fish Sauce, Baked Fish with Plum Tomatoes, Veracruz Red Snapper,* and *Steamed Salmon Steaks* served with the *Spicy Fish Sauce* or *Mustard-Yogurt Topping.* (Salmon, while not a low-fat fish, is especially low in cholesterol, and is permitted occasionally.)

Fish filets may also be cut into chunks for kebabs (see page 131) or for *Cioppino* or *Creamy Fish Chowder.*

Serve fish dishes with several lemon wedges, parsley, an oil-free salsa (our *Salsa* is a good one), *Spicy Fish Sauce,* or *Mustard-Yogurt Topping.*

Shellfish

Shrimp and crab are high in cholesterol, so these popular shellfish are permitted on the Pritikin diet in only half the usual portion allotments. However, other favorites, such as scallops, clams, oysters, and lobster, are permitted in the usual amounts.

Half a small broiled lobster, basted with lemon juice instead of butter and served with lemon wedges and bottled hot sauce, would be a good Pritikin entrée. Clams and oysters are suitable for chowder-type entrées (see "Main-Dish Soups," page 128), and a fine Italian-style entrée would be spaghetti or linguine with red clam sauce (without olive oil). Scallops could be used in a similar preparation.

Lobster and scallops are excellent prepared as kebabs, and in Chinese restaurants, lobster can be prepared Cantonese-style, omitting sesame oil and whole egg. Lobster or scallops, chopped or shredded, could be used in crêpes with a suitable sauce, or cut in chunks for main-dish salads (see page 124).

Experienced restaurateurs will undoubtedly create other ways of serving shellfish, Pritikin-style.

Meat—Low Food on the Totem Pole

Lean beef such as flank steak is permitted on the Pritikin diet, but red meat,* in general, tends to be too high in fat to be served in regular (3½-ounce) portions. Veal, sometimes thought to be nutritionally comparable to white meat chicken, is actually quite high in both fat and cholesterol, so is not favored. However, in small amounts—as a minor ingredient in recipes—beef, veal, and pork are acceptable.

Flank steak, a very lean cut of beef, is especially good in stir-fry Chinese preparations made with lots of vegetables and served with plenty of rice, such as *Tomato Beef Curry* and *Stir-Fried Steak and Green Peppers. Beef Stew,* made with lots of vegetables and potatoes and lean beef, and defatted before serving, is another option.

Other Entrées

Entrées such as stir-fry dishes, in which meat, poultry, fish, or shellfish are cut into small pieces and used together with

---

*Range-fed beef is much lower in fat than feedlot beef, but the range-fed form is not readily available to consumers.

other ingredients, especially vegetables and grains, are particularly suited to Pritikin meals, since a relatively small amount of animal food can flavor a large serving. Here are other popular entrées utilizing this approach that are easily tailored to meet Pritikin guidelines.

Kebabs

Since kebabs can be made with small amounts of animal food combined with lots of vegetables, this style of presenting fish, shellfish, or meat is suitable for Pritikin diners, accompanied by rice, rice pilaf, or a baked potato. Use lean chunks of fish, such as halibut or other white fish, lobster chunks or scallops, or thinly sliced flank steak, alternating with mushrooms, cherry tomatoes, and chunks of green pepper, onion, and, if desired, pineapple. Use oil-free marinades for the kebabs, basting while the kebabs are broiling.

"Edible Packages"

Whether the wrapping is a crêpe, a tortilla, cabbage leaves, or other food, "edible packages" are well suited to Pritikin guidelines. The stuffing may be vegetables, legumes, grains, meat, poultry, or shellfish, or a combination of some of these ingredients. A tasty sauce is often added that heightens the flavor. And the dish is usually accompanied by a grain or other complex-carbohydrate foods. A perfect Pritikin formula!

If using a crêpe wrapper, prepare a filling with chicken or crab meat or another shellfish. (In such small amounts, crab or shrimp are acceptable.) A good recipe is our *Crab or Chicken Crêpes with White Sauce.* (The recipe includes instructions for a Pritikin-acceptable crêpe wrapper.) The white sauce is made with evaporated skim milk, defatted chicken stock, white wine, and seasonings; if desired, mushrooms could be added.

Enchiladas, made with corn tortillas, are topped with zesty tomato sauces and filled with a variety of ingredients. Good enchilada recipes are our *Chicken or Turkey Enchiladas* and our low-calorie vegetarian *Eggplant Enchiladas.* Lean beef, beans, or skim-milk cottage cheese could also be used as the filling for delicious enchiladas.

Cabbage leaves or other leafy greens (romaine lettuce leaves, grape leaves, and so on) are the wrappers for very different kinds of fillings. Try *Sweet-Sour Cabbage Rolls,* filled with a rice-meat mixture and topped with a sweet-and-sour tomato sauce. Or make vegetarian versions with the alternate potato-grain filling, or with eggplant filling, using the *Stuffed Cabbage Rolls* recipe.

Mock Sour Cream is an attractive and tasty garnish for enchiladas and stuffed cabbage.

"Down Home" Recipes:
Chile con Carne, Spaghetti Sauce, and Meat Loaf

Popular, down-home recipes may also be adapted to Pritikin guidelines. Use very lean ground beef (preferably flank steak) or turkey, and skim off all fat that rises to the top of the cooking vessel.

Our chili con carne, *Turkey Chili,* is prepared by slowly simmering the cooked meat with kidney beans, tomatoes, onions, green peppers, and seasonings to develop robust flavor. It should be served over brown rice or whole-wheat pasta. Since the chili can be frozen and reheated, it is a particularly convenient restaurant item.

Spaghetti Sauce is delicious with a meat base or without it, vegetarian marinara-style. Like the chili, it can be frozen and reheated.

Or prepare *Meat-Rice Loaf,* served with a savory tomato sauce and accompanied by a baked potato or a baked sweet potato or yam.

Vegetable Stew and Curries

Besides the vegetarian recipes already mentioned, you may want to consider others. Piping hot *Vegetable Stew,* served in an individual crock and accompanied by our delicious *Corn Bread,* makes a very enjoyable meal. Customers with a taste for the exotic will relish *Vegetable Curry.* Serve it with an assortment of vegetable condiments and a dish of *Cucumbers with Yogurt,* made with nonfat yogurt and flavored with fresh mint. Customers preferring plain food will appreciate a plate of steamed vegetables, especially if they are on a weight-loss program. The vegetable plate could be enhanced by sautéing the vegetables (instead of steaming them) in defatted chicken stock and wine and seasoning them with herbs (fresh, if available) such as dill weed, thyme, and rosemary. A broiled tomato, sautéed mushrooms, and sliced cooked beets are good flavor and color accents for a basic vegetable plate of selected green and yellow vegetables.

Your selection of suitable vegetarian dishes can be augmented by others offered under "Side Dishes," discussed next.

Side Dishes

Raw or cooked vegetable dishes and potatoes, rice, and beans can be offered as side dishes, providing diners with an opportunity to assemble their own meals from this section of the menu or to augment their selections from other sections.

In addition to the usual basic dinner salad with a choice of dressings (see page 123 for a discussion of Pritikin dressings), why not offer Pritikin-style *Cole Slaw* and *Potato Salad?* The basic assorted relish tray (no olives, please; they are high-fat items) would also be a good choice for Pritikin diners. And Mexican restaurants (or restaurants opting for a bit of Mexican cuisine) could offer oven-toasted *Corn Chips,* served with *Salsa.* Another possible offering would be a tostada salad, created by oven-crisping a corn tortilla, spreading it with *"Refried" Beans* and *Salsa,* garnishing this with chopped vegetables (lettuce, tomato, green onions, and cilantro), and topping all with additional *Salsa* and *Mock Sour Cream.* The *"Refried" Beans* could also be offered by themselves, or with oven-toasted *Corn Chips* or steamed corn tortillas (for diners who wish to assemble their own tacos).

Spanish Rice is a good side dish to offer if the Mexican items just mentioned are being offered. *Herbed Rice Pilaf* would be an excellent complement to many dishes. But, at the minimum, offer these two: plain steamed brown rice and baked potatoes. The baked potato could be the most popular item in the side-order section. It should be served with *Mock Sour Cream* and chives. *Salsa* is also a nice accompaniment for baked potatoes.

Ratatouille, a classic French dish made by simmering diced eggplant with chopped onion, green pepper, and lots of tomato, is a good candidate for your side-order menu. It goes well with many entrées, or with just a baked potato or rice for a simple meal. Another very adaptable vegetable item to consider is corn on the cob. Fresh or frozen, corn is a fine complex-carbohydrate food that will go well with many orders.

Desserts

An assortment of fresh fruits—melon, berries, fresh fruit salad, or other choices—is the simplest Pritikin dessert repertoire, but if you are able to prepare them, some specialties would be very welcome. Consider *Creamy Tapioca Pudding, Apple-Raisin Pie* or blueberry- or cherry-topped *Buttermilk Chiffon Cheese Cake.* Many delicious recipes can be made to Pritikin guidelines. Another possibility would be to make a thin crêpe using whole-wheat flour, egg whites, and skimmed buttermilk; or use the recipe for crêpes in our *Crab or Chicken Crêpes with White Sauce.* Wrap the crêpe around some long, thin banana slices that have been sprinkled with a little lemon juice, and brown it on both sides in a nonstick skillet. Sprinkle cinnamon and a little apple juice over the crêpe while it is browning. Another delicious recipe is *Bananas in Berry Sauce,* which provides a simple but elegant fruit finale.

Breakfast Menu

Fresh fruit, whole-grain cereals, whole-grain breads, and whole-grain pancakes are the kinds of foods Pritikin-diet followers look for on breakfast menus. An excellent breakfast menu is the one offered by the Mana Kai Maui, reproduced on pages 100–101.

If the restaurateurs desire, the addition of egg dishes (made without yolks or fats) would be a special treat. These could include *French Toast,* made with whole-grain or sourdough bread, *Unscrambled Egg,* or an *Omelet.* Muffins and sweet breads made to Pritikin standards, such as *Apple-Oat Bran Muffins* and *Oatmeal Bread,* and fruit jams or hot fruit sauces like *Blueberry Jam* and *Hot Berry Sauce,* would be very special items also. Try serving the berry sauce over the whole-wheat crêpes or over *Buttermilk Pancakes* for a delicious breakfast dish.

Breads could include Pritikin whole-wheat, rye, or English muffins (or select comparable breads), and whole-wheat bagels.

If these suggestions have stimulated restaurateurs to consider more Pritikin-style items on their menus, we'll consider ourselves well rewarded. We can assure restaurateurs that Pritikin dieters are always on the lookout for menus that meet their needs particularly well.

Interested restaurateurs should also check the discussion in Chapter 1 for additional information that may be helpful.

We wish them well in their endeavors to offer the public more healthful alternatives when dining out.

List of Recipes for Restaurateurs

The following alphabetized list includes all recipes referred to in the preceding section for restaurateurs, together with a key for locating them in widely-available editions of previous books on the Pritikin Program in which they have appeared. A few of the recipes have not been published (as indicated by an asterisk in the right-hand column of the key), but these may be obtained directly from us by writing to: Pritikin Programs, P.O. Box 5335, Santa Barbara, CA 93108.

Letter designations for the books* used in the key are as follows:

PP   *The Pritikin Promise.* New York: Simon & Schuster, 1983. (hardback edition)

PPWLM   *The Pritikin Permanent Weight-Loss Manual.* New York: Bantam Books, 1982. (paperback edition)

PPDE   *The Pritikin Program for Diet & Exercise.*† New York: Bantam Books, 1982. (paperback edition)

---

*If you are using another edition of the same book, please use the recipe index in your book to find the recipe.

†In later books, recipes do not use black pepper (and white pepper, which is derived from black pepper), substituting instead cayenne or red pepper. Studies suggest that black pepper may be carcinogenic.

Recipe	Book(s) & Page Number(s)
Apple-Oat Bran Muffins	*PP* 301
Apple-Raisin Pie	*PP* 357–358
Baked Fish with Plum Tomatoes	*PP* 252–253
Bananas in Berry Sauce	*PP* 349
Beef Stew	*PPWLM* 269–270
Beet Borscht	*PPDE* 141
Blueberry Jam	*PP* 305
Breaded Fish	*PPWLM* 256
Breads and Breakfast Foods:	
Apple-Oat Bran Muffins	*PP* 301
Buttermilk Pancakes	*PPWLM* 321
Corn Bread	*PP* 208–209
French Toast	*PP* 304
Oatmeal Bread	*PP* 300–301
Omelet	*PPWLM* 284–285
Unscrambled Egg	*PP* 304–305
Buttermilk Chiffon Cheese Cake	*PPDE* 325
Buttermilk Pancakes	*PPWLM* 321
Cabbage Rolls, Stuffed	*PPWLM* 274–276
Cabbage Rolls, Sweet-Sour	*PP* 264–265
Carrot-Leek Soup	*PP* 201–202
Cheese Cake, Buttermilk Chiffon	*PPDE* 325
Chicken and Okra Gumbo	*PPWLM* 239–240
Chicken and Potatoes in Mushroom-Tomato Sauce	*PP* 210–211
Chicken Breasts aux Champignons	*PPWLM* 246–247
Chicken or Turkey Enchiladas	*PPWLM* 252–253
Chicken Salad	*
Chilled Cucumber Soup	*PP* 195
Chinese Sesame-Chicken Salad	*PP* 203
Cioppino	*PP* 286–287
Cole Slaw, Confetti Strip	*PPWLM* 210
Corn Bread	*PP* 208–209
Corn Chips	*PP* 336, *PPWLM* 348–349
Crab or Chicken Crêpes with White Sauce	*PPWLM* 259–260
Cranberry-Apple Compote	*PP* 270–271
Creamy Fish Chowder	*PP* 286
Creamy Fruit Salad	*PP* 324
Creamy Tapioca Pudding	*PP* 352–353
Crêpes	*PPWLM* 259–260, *PPDE* 247–248
Cucumber Soup, Chilled	*PP* 195
Cucumber-Yogurt Dressing	*PP* 343–344

Recipe	Book(s) & Page Number(s)
Cucumbers with Yogurt	*PP* 194–195
Desserts:	
Apple-Raisin Pie	*PP* 357–358
Bananas in Berry Sauce	*PP* 349
Buttermilk Chiffon Cheese Cake	*PPDE* 325
Creamy Tapioca Pudding	*PP* 352–353
Egg, Unscrambled	*PP* 304–305
Egg-Cheese Pâté	*PP* 316
Eggplant Enchiladas	*PPWLM* 283–284
Eight-Bean Soup	*PPDE* 281
Entrées:	
Baked Fish with Plum Tomatoes	*PP* 252–253
Beef Stew	*PPWLM* 269–270
Breaded Fish	*PPWLM* 256
Chicken and Potatoes in Mushroom-Tomato Sauce	*PP* 210–211
Chicken Breasts aux Champignons	*PPWLM* 246–247
Chicken or Turkey Enchiladas	*PPWLM* 252–253
Crab or Chicken Crêpes in White Sauce	*PPWLM* 259–260
Eggplant Enchiladas	*PPWLM* 283–284
Jade Empress Chicken	*PP* 202
Meat-Rice Loaf	*
Oven-Baked Breaded Chicken	*PP* 239
Oven-Baked Breaded Filet of Sole	*PP* 198
Ratatouille	*PPWLM* 290–292, 249
Sri Lanka Chicken Curry	*PP* 248
Steamed Salmon Steaks	*PP* 273
Stir-Fried Steak and Green Peppers	*PPWLM* 265
Stuffed Breast of Chicken with Lemon-Wine Sauce	*PPWLM* 245–246
Stuffed Cabbage Rolls	*PPWLM* 274–276
Sweet-Sour Cabbage Rolls	*PP* 264–265
Tomato Beef Curry	*PPWLM* 265–266
Turkey Breast Slices in Wine-Caper Sauce	*PP* 267
Turkey Chili	*PP* 207–208
Turkey "Fried" Steak	*PP* 238–239
Turkey Tetrazzini	*
Vegetable Curry	*PP* 193–194
Vegetable Stew	*PP* 229
Veracruz Red Snapper	*PP* 253

Recipe	Book(s) & Page Number(s)
Fish, Baked, with Plum Tomatoes	*PP* 252–253
Fish Dressing	*PPWLM* 354
French Dressing	*PP* 341
"French Fries"	*PP* 315
French Toast	*PP* 304
Garbanzo Minestrone	*PP* 242
Gazpacho	*PP* 289–290
Greek Salad	*PPWLM* 209
Hearty Lentil Soup	*PP* 232
Herbed Rice Pilaf	*PPWLM* 328
Hot Berry Sauce	*PP* 308
Jade Empress Chicken	*PP* 202
Lentil Soup	*PPDE* 278–279
Linguine Salad	*PP* 237
Mashed Potatoes	*PP* 199
Meat-Rice Loaf	*
Mock Sour Cream	*PP* 345–346, *PPWLM* 355, *PPDE* 313
Mustard-Yogurt Topping	*PP* 344
Nonfat Yogurt	*PP* 346–347, *PPWLM* 356–357
Oatmeal Bread	*PP* 300–301
Omelet	*PPWLM* 284–285
Oven-Baked Breaded Chicken	*PP* 239
Oven-Baked Breaded Filet of Sole	*PP* 198
Pickle Relish	*PP* 328–329
Pickled Cucumbers	*PP* 329
Pie, Apple-Raisin	*PP* 357–358
Pimiento Cheese	*PP* 317
Potato Salad	*PP* 320–321
Potatoes, Mashed	*PP* 199
Ratatouille	*PPWLM* 290–292, 249
Red Snapper, Veracruz	*PP* 253
"Refried" Beans	*PPWLM* 306–307
Salad Dressings and Toppings:	*PP* 341–346, *PPWLM* 218–226
Cucumber-Yogurt Dressing	*PP* 343–344
Fish Dressing	*PPWLM* 354
French Dressing	*PP* 341
Mock Sour Cream	*PP* 345–346, *PPWLM* 355, *PPDE* 313
Mustard-Yogurt Topping	*PP* 344
Nonfat Yogurt	*PP* 346–347, *PPWLM* 356–357
Pickle Relish	*PP* 328–329

Recipe	Book(s) & Page Number(s)
Salsa	*PP* 345
Spicy Fish Sauce	*PP* 198
Vinaigrette Dressing	*PP* 341
Zesty Tomato Dressing	*PP* 342
Salads:	
Chicken Salad	*
Chinese Sesame-Chicken Salad	*PP* 203
Cole Slaw, Confetti Strip	*PPWLM* 210
Creamy Fruit Salad	*PP* 324
Greek Salad	*PPWLM* 209
Linguine Salad	*PP* 237
Potato Salad	*PP* 320–321
Tabbouli Salad	*PP* 325
Tuna Salad	*PP* 326
Tuna-Linguine Salad	*PP* 237
Salmon Pâté	*PP* 316
Salmon Steaks, Steamed	*PP* 273
Salsa	*PP* 345
Sandwich Spreads and Toppings:	
Blueberry Jam	*PP* 305
Cranberry-Apple Compote	*PP* 270–271
Egg-Cheese Pâté	*PP* 316
Hot Berry Sauce	*PP* 308
Pimiento Cheese	*PP* 317
Salmon Pâté	*PP* 316
Sole, Oven-Baked Breaded Filet of	*PP* 198
Soups:	*PPWLM* 227–244
Beet Borscht	*PPDE* 141
Carrot-Leek Soup	*PP* 201–202
Chicken and Okra Gumbo	*PPWLM* 239–240
Chilled Cucumber Soup	*PP* 195
Chinese Tomato-Vegetable Soup	*PPWLM* 228–229
Cioppino	*PP* 286–287
Creamy Fish Chowder	*PP* 286
Eight-Bean Soup	*PPDE* 281
Garbanzo Minestrone	*PP* 242
Gazpacho	*PP* 289–290
Hearty Lentil Soup	*PP* 232
Lentil Soup	*PPDE* 278–279
Split Pea Soup	*PPDE* 278
Tomato Bouillon	*PP* 234–235
Tomato-Okra Soup	*PPWLM* 228
Tomato-Rice Soup	*PPDE* 142–143
Vegetable-Barley Soup	*PP* 261
White Bean-and-Turkey Soup	*PP* 260–261

Recipe	Book(s) & Page Number(s)
Sour Cream, Mock	*PP* 345–346, *PPWLM* 355, *PPDE* 313
Spaghetti Sauce	*
Spanish Rice	*PP* 232–233
Spicy Fish Sauce	*PP* 198
Split Pea Soup	*PPDE* 278
Sri Lanka Chicken Curry	*PP* 248
Steamed Salmon Steaks	*PP* 273
Stir-Fried Steak and Green Peppers	*PPWLM* 265
Stuffed Breast of Chicken with Lemon-Wine Sauce	*PPWLM* 245–246
Stuffed Cabbage Rolls	*PPWLM* 274–276
Sweet-Sour Cabbage Rolls	*PP* 264–265
Tabbouli Salad	*PP* 325
Tapioca Pudding, Creamy	*PP* 352–353
Tomato Beef Curry	*PPWLM* 265–266
Tomato Bouillon	*PP* 234–235
Tomato-Okra Soup	*PPWLM* 228
Tomato-Rice Soup	*PPDE* 142–143
Tuna Salad	*PP* 326
Tuna-Linguine Salad	*PP* 237
Turkey Breast Slices in Wine-Caper Sauce	*PP* 267
Turkey Chili	*PP* 207–208
Turkey "Fried" Steak	*PP* 238–239
Turkey Tetrazzini	*
Unscrambled Egg	*PP* 304–305
Vegetable-Barley Soup	*PP* 261
Vegetable Curry	*PP* 193–194
Vegetable Stew	*PP* 229
Veracruz Red Snapper	*PP* 253
Vinaigrette Dressing	*PP* 341
White Bean-and-Turkey Soup	*PP* 260–261
Yogurt, Nonfat	*PP* 346–347, *PPWLM* 356–357
Zesty Tomato Dressing	*PP* 342

8

Some Restaurants at Which You Can Order Pritikin Meals

The following restaurant names were submitted to us by faithful Pritikinites who have dined in these establishments and were satisfied. Although we cannot endorse any of these restaurants outright, we would like to share these suggestions with you.

Each restaurant listed has provided us with detailed information about their menu items, atmosphere, and considerations for special food preparation. All the descriptions have been verified by each restaurant, but you may wish to call ahead in the event changes may have occurred.

Note that for your convenience, each restaurant is described with an approximate price evaluation coded as: "$" for moderately priced and "$$" for expensive. "B," "L," and "D" represent breakfast, lunch, and dinner, respectively.

Please let us know of other restaurants you have discovered that meet your Pritikin-style dining needs, so that we can include them in future guides. Also, let us hear from you on your experiences at the restaurants we have listed. Use the forms on pages 191–198, and send all comments to Restaurant Guide, Pritikin Programs. P.O. Box 5335, Santa Barbara, CA 93108.

HAPPY DINING!

ARIZONA

PHOENIX

Hunan Restaurant
Sam Lee, Manager
1575 E. Camelback
Phoeniz, AZ 85014
602-265-9484

Call ahead for reservations—specify that Pritikin preparation is required. Ask for Sam Lee. All dishes can be made without salt, oil, or MSG. Spiciness modified to taste. Specialties include Buddha's Delight and corn soup. Can add chicken breast, fish, or lean red beef, if desired. L$, D$, Chinese.

TUCSON

Rose Garden
Carol Ong, Manager
3001 N. Campbell Ave.
Tucson, AZ 85705
602-327-5055

No advance notice is necessary. Request no salt, MSG, oil, or sugar. Over 100 dishes, including all-vegetable dishes and tofu. Uses only lean red meat, skinless chicken, and fresh vegetables. L$, D$, Chinese.

The Solarium
Bill MacMorran, Frank Wood,
Dan Chriszt, Lois Thornberg, Managers
6444 E. Tanque Verde
Tucson, AZ 85715
602-886-8186

An artistic statement in wood and glass, in sun and light-metal sculptures, inlaid tile mosaics, to the tiniest flower in the center of your table. Features fowl, fresh fish, oysters, and other seafood specialties. When making reservations, ask for the manager and indicate your dietary needs. L$, D$$, fine restaurant.

CALIFORNIA

BURBANK

Full O Life Foods, Inc.
Edward B. Matheson, Manager
2515 W. Magnolia Blvd.
Burbank, CA 91505
213-845-8343

Features two vegetarian entrées and chicken and fish entrées daily. Baked potatoes and baked yams starting at 11 AM every day. Full variety of salads. All vegetables are fresh. Whole-grain pastas and breads. Herb teas. L$, D$, family restaurant.

CALABASAS

Calabasas Inn
Sandy Leslie, Manager
23500 Park Sorrento Dr.
Calabasas, CA 91302
213-888-8870

No MSG used. Chef is Pritikin fan. Menu features fresh fish and vegetables. L$, D$, fine restaurant.

CANOGA PARK

Follow Your Heart
Kathy Holm, Manager
21825 Sherman Way
Canoga Park, CA 91303
213-348-3240

Offers cold steamed vegetable salad, mixed raw vegetable salad, garden salad, steamed brown rice, fresh steamed vegetable plate, herb teas. L$, D$, vegetarian.

DAVIS

Blue Mango
Walter H. Smith, Manager
330 G St.
Davis, CA 95616
916-756-2616

Corn tortillas made without oil, salt, or sugar. In winter a 9-grain hot cereal. Fruit salad or melon plate (seasonal). Request "no oil" when ordering sautéed vegetables or dinner-entrée vegetables. Call ahead to ask about lunch or dinner specials and to request pita whole-wheat bread. Happy to accommodate special diets, especially if you can give one-day advance notice. B$, L$, D$, family restaurant.

EL CAJON

L'Chaim Restaurant
Garry A. Flam, Manager
134 W. Douglas
El Cajon, CA 92020
619-442-1331

Stir-fry rice (in broth, not oil), tofu vegetable scramble, vegetable platters, salads, daily special entrées. Advise waitperson of dietary requirements—very accommodating. L$, D$, vegetarian restaurant.

HOLLYWOOD

Nucleus Nuance Restaurant
Bruce & Katherine Veniero, Managers
7267 Melrose Ave.
West Hollywood, CA 90046
213-939-8666

Happy to comply with special diets. Vegetable and fruit salads, broiled fish, skinned and broiled chicken. L$$, D$$, fine restaurant.

LAGUNA HILLS

Grand Shanghai Restaurant
Ming Chun Cha, Manager
25381 Alicia Pkwy.
Laguna Hills, CA 92653
714-951-1981

No advance notice necessary. Dishes cooked to order. L$, D$, Chinese restaurant.

LOS ANGELES

The Artful Balance
Rinda Lander & Calvin Lazarus, Managers
525½ N. Fairfax Ave.
Los Angeles, CA 90036
213-852-9091

Vegetable and fruit salads, baked potatoes, broiled or poached fish, steamed vegetables, sourdough, pita, and whole-wheat bread, dinner salads, oil-free salad dressings, oil/lard-free refried beans, no MSG or salt. D$, family restaurant.

Chicken Natural Restaurant
Phil Orlow, Manager
11070 Santa Monica Blvd.
West Los Angeles, CA 90025
213-473-2169

All natural foods, all salads, skewered chicken in a special salt- and oil-free mixture with herbs and natural spices. L$, D$, fast-food restaurant.

Ciao Giuseppe
Giuseppe Bellisario, Manager
8256 Beverly Blvd.
Los Angeles, CA 90048
213-653-8025

No advance notice necessary. Advise maître d' or waiter of Pritikin requirements. L$$, D$$, fine Italian restaurant.

Golden Temple Conscious Cookery
RanBir Singh Bhai, Manager
7910 W. 3rd St.
Los Angeles, CA 90048
213-655-1891

No advance notice necessary. Absolutely no eggs, no sugar, and no preservatives. Vegetable entrées, salads. L$, D$, vegetarian restaurant.

Hampton's
Dana Harden, Manager
1342 N. Highland Ave.
Los Angeles, CA 90028
213-469-1090

Familiar with serving Pritikin customers. Salad bar, steamed vegetables *al dente*. Sourdough bread can be ordered plain. Homemade vegetable soup made without salt, MSG, or beef base. L$, D$, family restaurant.

Matteo's Restaurant
Michael Jordan, Manager
2321 Westwood Blvd.
Los Angeles, CA 90064
213-475-4521

Pasta dishes cooked with no salt. Fresh tomato sauce cooked with no salt or oil—includes fresh basil, onions, garlic, mushrooms. Skinless chicken cacciatore, prepared with no salt or oil, with mushrooms, peppers, and onions. Steamed fresh white fish cooked with shredded vegetables or plain broiled white fish with a touch of fresh lemon. No advance notice necessary for above dishes. Just ask for Mike or Jimmy and say you are on the Pritikin diet. D$$, fine restaurant.

Paul's Juice & Salad Bar
Paul Bisbano, Manager
6333 W. 3rd St.
Los Angeles, CA 90036
213-937-9360

A specialized fast-food restaurant in the Farmers Market. Offer 9 fresh fruit salads year round. B$, L$, D$, fast-food restaurant.

MISSION VIEJO

Papa Cha
Ming Chun Cha, Manager
24501 Marguerite Pkwy.
Mission Viejo, CA 92675
714-951-7771

No advance notice necessary. Food cooked to order. L$, D$, fast-food drive-up Chinese restaurant.

PALM SPRINGS

Jeremiah's
Tony Mancini, Manager
1201 E. Palm Canyon
Palm Springs, CA 92262
619-327-1469

Vegetable and fruit salad bars, baked potatoes, broiled or poached fish, steamed vegetables, marinara sauce, sourdough bread, pita bread, whole-wheat bread, dinner salads, skinned chicken breast. No MSG or salt. Will sauté in broth. Call to have your name put on the waiting list 2 hours in advance of the time you would like to dine (Palm Springs only). D$$, chain restaurant.

Lam's Garden Chinese Restaurant
Samuel Lam, Manager
622 N. Palm Canyon Dr.
Palm Springs, CA 92262
619-325-8860

22 dishes can be prepared Pritikin-style, upon request. No advance notice necessary. D$, family Chinese restaurant.

Soo's Kitchen
Sandra Soo, Manager
394 N. Palm Canyon Dr.
Palm Springs, CA 92262
619-325-0868

Call ahead for special preparation and ask Sandra for Pritikin dishes. Stir-fry fresh vegetables, no oil, no salt, no MSG, with or without skinless chicken breast. L$, D$, family Chinese restaurant.

PALO ALTO

Fish Market Restaurant
Various locations in
Palo Alto, Santa Clara, San Mateo, CA

Ask for dishes salt-free and oil-free upon ordering. Steamed vegetable plate always available. Broiled fish. Oil-free dressing made with yogurt, cucumber, and garlic. L$, D$, family restaurant, seafood only.

PASADENA

Beadle's Cafeteria
Jane Arvizu, Ed Clinton,
  Manuel Gordon, Carolyn Artman, Managers
850 E. Colorado Blvd.
Pasadena, CA 91101
213-796-3618

Baked fish any time. Fresh turkey on Tuesdays. 9–12 vegetables on our counter every day (some fresh, some frozen), fresh fruit, always fresh lettuce salads. L$, D$, family restaurant.

Benson's Bar & Grill
Stephen Francis, Manager
424 Fair Oaks
S. Pasadena, CA 91030
213-799-0857

No advance notice necessary. Baked potatoes, steamed vegetables, broiled or poached fish. L$, D$$, family restaurant.

The Chronicle
R. K. Erickson, Manager
897 Granite Dr.
Pasadena, CA 91101
213-792-1179

San Francisco bar-and-grill atmosphere. Meals prepared to order and served with the freshest of vegetables. Pritikin Program meals need only be requested by specific mention to the management. Chicken can be broiled to your request. Fresh fish poached or broiled. Clams, oysters, shrimps, and crab served fresh over ice. L$$, D$$, fine restaurant.

SAN DIEGO

Souplantation
Mark Bayerle, Manager
3960 W. Pt. Loma Blvd.
San Diego, CA 92110
619-222-7404

No sulfiting agents used on salad bar items. Seats 150–200. L$, D$, self-service restaurant.

Yet Wah
Michael Wong, Manager
3146 Sports Arena Blvd.
San Diego, CA 92110
619-223-9800

No advance notice necessary. Dishes cooked to order. Steamed vegetables. L$, D$$, fine Mandarin Chinese restaurant.

SAN MATEO

Fish Market Restaurant
Various locations in
San Mateo, Santa Clara, Palo Alto, CA

Ask for dishes salt-free and oil-free upon ordering. Steamed vegetable plate always available. Broiled fish. Oil-free dressing made with yogurt, cucumber, and garlic. L$, D$, family restaurant, seafood only.

SANTA CLARA

Fish Market Restaurant
Various locations in
Santa Clara, San Mateo, Palo Alto, CA

Ask for dishes salt-free and oil-free upon ordering. Steamed vegetable plate always available. Broiled fish. Oil-free dressing made with yogurt, cucumber, and garlic. L$, D$, family restaurant, seafood only.

SANTA MONICA

Madame Wu's Garden
Madame Wu, Manager
2201 Wilshire Blvd.
Santa Monica, CA 90403
213-828-5656

Madame Wu has 6 dishes on her menu that follow Pritikin guidelines. Call ahead for special preparation. L$, D$$, fine Chinese restaurant.

Pier II Fish Broiler
Berha Huang, Manager
1104 Wilshire Bldg.
Santa Monica, CA 90401
213-393-0447

Everything can be specially prepared for your dietary needs. No oil and/or no salt. No advance notice necessary. Let your waiter or waitress know when you order. Fresh fish, salad bar. L$, D$–$$, fine family restaurant.

SEAL BEACH

Rappazzini's Pure 'n Simple
John Rappazzini, Manager
115 Main St.
Seal Beach, CA 90740
213-430-4540

Most foods cooked without oil or butter. No salt, sugar, or honey. Salad bar, soups, baked potatoes or yams, brown rice, whole-wheat pastas, vegetables, meat and vegetarian dishes, oil-free salad dressings and marinara sauce, skinned chicken. B$, L$, D$, fine restaurant.

SHERMAN OAKS

Chung King Inn
John Lee, Manager
14010 Ventura Blvd.
Sherman Oaks, CA 91403
213-783-9046

No advance notice necessary. All entrées cooked to order. Regularly serves people (including groups) on the Pritikin diet. Pritikin choices include hot-and-sour soup, curry chicken, vegetarian delite, and kung pao chicken (or shrimp). D$, family restaurant.

La Frite
Patrick Herron, Manager
15013 Ventura Blvd.
Sherman Oaks, CA 91403
213-990-1791

Fresh fruit salads, grilled fresh fish, vegetables to order. L$, D$$, French café.

L'Express
John Robinson, Guy Claisy, Managers
14910 Ventura Blvd.
Sherman Oaks, CA 91403
213-990-8683

Salads, fresh fruit salads, grilled fresh fish served without any sauce, vegetables to order. B$, L$, D$$, French café.

SOLANA BEACH

The Fish Market
Dean Betts, John Freis, Managers
640 Via de la Valle
Solana Beach, CA 92075
619-755-2277

Ask for dishes salt-free/oil-free upon ordering. Broiled fish. Steamed vegetable plate always available. Oil-free dressing made with yogurt, cucumber, and garlic. L$, D$, family restaurant, seafood only.

STUDIO CITY

Chez Natural
Alex Reuss, Manager
11838 Ventura Blvd.
Studio City, CA 91604
213-763-1044

No advance notice necessary. Fresh fruit salad, home-baked breads. No sugar, artificial sweeteners, preservatives, flavor enhancers, or artificial chemicals of any kind. All entrées served with fresh vegetables or fresh fruit. Chicken and fish available. Caring atmosphere. L$, D$$, fine vegetarian restaurant.

THOUSAND OAKS

Pelican's Wharf
Edgar Wootton, Manager
1352 Moorpark Rd.
Thousand Oaks, CA 91360
805-497-7595

25-item fresh salad bar. 5 fresh fish items each day—can be broiled dry. No salt used. No objection to sharing entrées. Very flexible. Ask for Ed. D$–$$, fine restaurant.

VENICE

Figtree's Cafe
William Feigenbaum, Manager
429 Ocean Front Walk
Venice, CA 90291
213-392-4937

Whole grains, fresh fish, organically-raised chicken, bakery with whole-grain items, extensive salad menu. Features complete dinners usually with 2 choices of soup (vegetarian) and steamed vegetables. Fresh fish, broiled chicken, tofu brochette, herbal teas. No advance notice necessary, but any dish can be prepared by calling ahead. B$, L$, D$, fine vegetarian restaurant.

WOODLAND HILLS

Sage Natural Foods
Donna Wilson, Manager
21837 Ventura Blvd.
Woodland Hills, CA 91364
213-992-5979

Deli—take out or eat here. Soups made without oil. No dairy. Salads, lard-free refried beans, whole-grain breads, oil-free salad dressings. L$, D$, vegetarian self-service restaurant.

CONNECTICUT

BRIDGEPORT

Bloodroot, Ltd.
Betsey Beaven, Noel Giordano,
*   Selma Miriam, Patricia Shea, Managers*
85 Ferris St.
Bridgeport, CT 06605
203-576-9168

Extensive vegetarian menu including entirely dairy-free dishes. Menu changes every few weeks. Unable to prepare any dishes to special order except salads; however, always seem to have food acceptable to Pritikin followers. No MSG or artificial seasonings. Oil and salt used in moderation. Each salad is made to order. L$, D$, self-service vegetarian restaurant.

NORWALK

Lime Restaurant
Vincent Cabozzetta, Manager
168 Main St.
Norwalk, CT 06851
203-846-9240

Hearty tofu pita-bread sandwiches, meatless stocks in all soups, breast of chicken, fresh fish, whole-grain breads. Specify dietary requirements when ordering. Butter and some other dairy products can be omitted from dishes. Some special dishes can be made at off-peak times. L$, D$, family restaurant.

STAMFORD

Sai Wu
Bernard Leung, Manager
109 Atlantic St.
Stamford, CT 06901
203-348-3330

Steamed vegetables, chicken, oil- and egg-free noodles. Specializes in Buddha's Delight. No advance notice necessary. Dishes cooked to order. L$, D$$, fine Cantonese-Szechuan restaurant.

FLORIDA

CORAL GABLES

Spiral Restaurant
Jerry Goldschein, Manager
1630 Ponce DeLeon Blvd.
Coral Gables, FL 33134
305-446-1591

Fresh salads, such as "chef in the raw," and our far-out fruit platter served any time. Two of our house specialties can be made without oil, upon request. L$, D$, vegetarian restaurant.

MIAMI

Cafe Mendocino
Michael Compton, Manager
5950 Sunset Dr.
S. Miami, FL 33143
305-666-7911

Whole grains, beans, daily fresh vegetables, and fresh (not frozen) seafood are basis for menu items. B$, L$, D$, family vegetarian restaurant.

Granny Feelgoods
Irving Fields, Manager
190 S.E. 1st Ave.
Miami, FL 33131
305-358-6233

Vegetable and fruit salad bars, baked potatoes, broiled or poached fish, steamed vegetables. Will sauté in broth. B$, L$, D$, restaurant and store.

Great House on the Bay
Irving Bakst, Manager
Towers of Quayside
5000 Towerside Terr.
Miami, FL 33138
305-893-2345

Salads, baked potatoes, steamed vegetables, whole-wheat pasta and bread, oil-free marinara sauce, skinned chicken breast, poached fish. Call ahead for special preparation. L$, D$, fine restaurant.

Here Comes the Sun
Selwyn Medin, Manager
2188 N.E. 123 St.
N. Miami, FL 33181
305-893-5711

No advance notice necessary. Omelets (white of egg only) with mushrooms or onions, vegetarian plate with salad, rice, vegetables, beans, lasagna with hoop and sapsago cheeses, broiled fish of the day, steamed julienne vegetables with tofu or rice, breast of chicken, artichoke pasta. L$, D$, family restaurant.

Natural Eats
Lawrence S. Rosenberg, Manager
9477 S. Dixie Hwy.
Miami, FL 33156
305-665-7807

Variety of salads, fresh fruit medley, pita bread, and bagels. B$, L$, family restaurant.

Unicorn Restaurant
Terry Dalton, Manager
16454 N.E. 6th Ave.
N. Miami Beach, FL 33162
305-944-5595

80% of menu can be ordered without oil or salt. All-natural dessert bar, oil-free soups. B$, L$, D$, family vegetarian restaurant.

Wah Shing
Alfred Worton, Manager
9503 S. Dixie Hwy.
Miami, FL 33156
305-667-9294

Offers over 26 kinds of vegetables from its organic farm in W. Palm Beach. Uses defatted chicken broth. Shrimp and lobster come from the north on ice, not frozen. Fish is from the Keys. Can cook fish, seafood, vegetables with different styles of Chinese cooking. L$, D$, family Chinese restaurant.

PALM BEACH

Maurice's Italian Restaurant
John Smigel, Manager
191 Bradley Pl.
Palm Beach, FL 33480
305-832-1843

.Several entrées especially for Pritikin diners, including eggplant Milanese, spaghetti primavera, catch of the day, chicken printanier. All dinners served with house salad and hot bread. L$, D$, Italian restaurant.

SARASOTA

House of Chong
Jerry Ginnis, Manager
6914 S. Tamiami Trail
Sarasota, FL 33581
813-922-4446

Most of menu is cooked to order. Can cook without salt, sugar, MSG, oil, or whatever customer wishes. No advance notice necessary. L$, D$, Chinese restaurant.

GEORGIA

ATLANTA

Souper Salad Franchises
14 locations in Atlanta, GA;
LaFayette, LA; and Austin,
Dallas, and Houston, TX

Fresh, uncooked, unseasoned, untreated vegetables on 60-item salad bar. Iceberg and romaine lettuce, spinach, carrots, celery, radishes, cucumbers, yellow squash, zucchini, broccoli, cauliflower, cherry tomatoes, mushrooms, green peppers, red onions, and alfalfa sprouts. L$, D$, chain restaurant.

HAWAII

MAUI

The Ocean Terrace Restaurant
J. Randol Christman, Manager
Mana Kai Maui Condominium/Hotel
2960 S. Kihei Rd.
Kihei, Maui, HI 96753
808-879-2607

See pages 100–103 for Mana Kai Maui Pritikin-style breakfast menu and discussion. Restaurant also serves Pritikin-style lunch and dinner as well as conventional meals. B$, L$, D$–$$, family hotel restaurant.

ILLINOIS

CHICAGO

Blackhawk Restaurant
Don Roth, Manager
110 E. Pearson St.
Chicago, IL 60611
312-726-0100

Salad bar, baked potatoes, broiled or poached fish, steamed vegetables, dinner salads, wine vinegar, chicken breast. Can sauté in broth. Call ahead for special orders. Reservations necessary. L$, D$$, family restaurant.

Ciel Bleu
Pierre Robert, Manager
Mayfair Regent Hotel
181 E. Lake Shore Dr.
Chicago, IL 60611
312-787-8500

Rolled oats, shredded wheat, fresh fruit, poached fresh fish, skinless chicken, salads, steamed vegetables, pita bread, wild rice, spaghettini primavera. Call ahead for special preparations. B$$, L$$, D$$, fine restaurant.

Heather House
Carson Pirie Scott & Co.
1 S. State St.
Chicago, IL 60603
312-744-2134

Salad circle, baked potatoes, steamed vegetables, fresh fruit, turkey sandwich, pita bread. L$, D$$, fine restaurant. Dinner served Monday and Thursday evenings only—4:30 to 6:30.

Hunan Palace
Peter Hou, Manager
1050 N. State St.
Chicago, IL 60611
312-642-1800

Features Chinese salad, steamed pike. All dishes made to order. Ask maître d' to modify dishes. L$, D$$, gourmet Chinese restaurant.

Kamehachi of Tokyo
Ben Fujii, Manager
1617 N. Wells
Chicago, IL 60614
312-664-3663

Authentic Japanese food, sushi bar, salads, steamed vegetables, salmon, trout, skinless chicken breast, yam vermicelli. Advance notice required. Call for reservations. L$$, D$$, fine restaurant.

Szechwan House
Simon Lin, Manager
600 N. Michigan Ave.
Chicago, IL 60611
312-642-3900

No advance notice necessary. Many vegetable dishes. L$, D$, fine Chinese restaurant.

HINSDALE

The Cypress
Sean Hartney, Manager
500 E. Ogden
Hinsdale, IL 60521
312-323-2727

Controlled portion sizes. Adjusted cooking procedures. Special orders usually available upon request. Fresh fish daily, skinned chicken, steamed vegetables, baked potatoes. L$, D$, fine restaurant.

LINCOLNWOOD

Myron & Phil
Myron Freedman, Phil Freedman, Managers
3900 W. Devon Ave.
Lincolnwood, IL 60645
312-677-6663

Myron Freedman is an alumni of the Santa Barbara Pritikin Center. Available to Pritikin dieters: salt-free steamed vegetables, broiled fish, chicken, bread, salad dressing. L$, D$, fine restaurant.

SKOKIE

La Salade
Peggy Luther, Manager
3938 W. Dempster
Skokie, IL 60076
312-679-6190

Included in the buffet selection are various fresh fruits and vegetables. Hot dishes: brown rice, tofu, broiled chicken, boiled potatoes. Friday, Saturday, Sunday—poached salmon and poached trout. L$, D$, self-service restaurant.

LOUISIANA

CHALMETTE

Spectacular Tubers
Mike Sherwood, Manager
8913 W. Judge Perez
Chalmette, LA 70043
504-277-2727

Salad bar, baked potatoes, steamed vegetables, sourdough bread, pita bread, dinner salads, wine vinegar, chicken breast, pocket-bread sandwiches. Take out or eat in. L$, D$, fast-food chain restaurant.

HARVEY

Spectacular Tubers
Donna Lee, Manager
2209 LaPalco
Harvey, LA 70058
504-362-4464

Salad bar, baked potatoes, steamed vegetables, sourdough bread, pita bread, dinner salads, wine vinegar, chicken breast, pocket-bread sandwiches. Take out or eat in. L$, D$, fast-food chain restaurant.

LAFAYETTE

Souper Salad Franchises
14 locations in LaFayette, LA;
Atlanta, GA; and Austin, Dallas,
and Houston, TX

Fresh, uncooked, unseasoned, untreated vegetables on 60-item salad bar. Iceberg and romaine lettuce, spinach, carrots, celery, radishes, cucumbers, yellow squash, zucchini, broccoli, cauliflower, cherry tomatoes, mushrooms, green peppers, red onions, and alfalfa sprouts. L$, D$, chain restaurant.

MANDEVILLE

Trey Yuen
Tom Wong, Manager
600 N. Causeway
Mandeville, LA 70448
504-626-4476

Will cook to order. No advance notice necessary. D$$, fine Chinese restaurant.

METAIRIE

Randall's Restaurant
Randy Osborne, Manager
3044 Ridgelake Dr.
Metairie, LA 70002
504-834-8928

Baked potatoes, broiled or poached fish, steamed vegetables, dinner salads, oil-free salad dressings, chicken breast. Can sauté in broth. Reservations required for dinner. Open 7 days, will Pritikinize dishes. L$, D$$, fine seafood restaurant.

Spectacular Tubers
Gary Ricks, Manager
2609 Harvard Ave.
Metairie, LA 70002
504-455-3250

Salad bar, baked potatoes, steamed vegetables, sourdough bread, pita bread, dinner salads, wine vinegar, chicken breast, pocket-bread sandwiches. Take out or eat in. L$, D$, fast-food chain restaurant.

Taj Mahal Cuisine of India
Har Keswani, Manager
1521 Causeway Blvd.
Metairie, LA 70001
504-833-3456

Call in advance for special preparation. Will make anything Pritikin-style with notice. No MSG or additives. Will make whole-wheat Pritikin bread—notify in advance. L$, D$$, fine authentic Indian restaurant.

NEW ORLEANS

The Andrew Jackson Restaurant
Jay Sevin, Manager
221 Royal Dr.
New Orleans, LA 70130
504-529-2603

Reservations suggested. Special dishes made to order. Baked potatoes, broiled or poached fish, dinner salads, wine vinegar, chicken breast. Can sauté in broth. L$$, D$$, fine French restaurant.

Antoine's
Roy F. Gust, Jr., Manager
713 Rue St. Louis
New Orleans, LA 70112
504-581-4422

Baked potatoes, broiled fish, steamed vegetables, dinner salads, wine vinegar, chicken breast. Reservations needed. Call ahead for special orders. L$$, D$$, fine French restaurant.

The Chart House
Syril Schwartz, Manager
801 Chartres St.
New Orleans, LA 70116
504-523-2015

Baked potatoes, broiled fish, steamed vegetables, dinner salads, wine vinegar. First come, first served. Call in advance for special orders. D$$, fine restaurant.

Imperial Palace Regency
Lorraine Lee, Manager
601 Loyola Ave.
New Orleans, LA 70112
504-522-8666

Reservations recommended. Will make accommodations for those following Pritikin diet. Poached fish, steamed vegetables, chicken breast, wine vinegar. Can sauté in broth. L$$, D$$, fine gourmet Chinese restaurant.

MaiTai
Ken Mui, Manager
5796 Crowder Blvd.
New Orleans, LA 70127
504-246-9998

No advance notice necessary. Reservations needed at lunch. Dishes cooked to order. L$, D$, family Chinese restaurant.

Nature's Way Salad Shop
Conrad Ingold, Manager
5932 Magazine St.
New Orleans, LA 70115
504-897-0511

No advance notice needed. Steamed vegetables, dinner salads, sourdough bread. Some foods can be made oil-free and salt-free. Good for vegetables, salads, and grains. L$, D$, family vegetarian restaurant.

The Riverview
Peggy Kalinski, Manager
Marriott Hotel
41st Fl.
555 Canal St.
New Orleans, LA 70140
504-581-1000

Baked potatoes, broiled or poached fish, steamed vegetables, dinner salads. Can sauté in broth. Reservations recommended. Won table-top award—nationally recognized. Sunday brunch has fresh vegetables and fruits. Will cook with special consideration for those on Pritikin diet, with advance notice. D$$, fine continental restaurant.

ZaZou
Barry Herman, Manager
3442 St. Charles Ave.
New Orleans, LA 70115
504-895-4400

Call for reservations, seating is limited. Baked potatoes, poached fish, steamed vegetables. Can sauté in broth. Oil-free marinara sauce, pita bread, dinner salads, oil-free salad dressing, Irish oatmeal, whole-wheat pasta. Excellent restaurant for Pritikin meals. Has whole-wheat croissants and a variety of Pritikin foods. Catering available. B$, L$, D$$, fine continental restaurant.

MARYLAND

BETHESDA

Asti-Roseto Restaurant
Frank Lantella, Manager
7940 Wisconsin Ave.
Bethesda, MD 20814
301-652-1300

Call ahead for any special preparation—ask for Frank or Martha Lantella. Fresh tomato sauce—be sure to mention not to use oil when preparing. Luncheon buffet includes salads. For dinner try a pasta dish or broiled filet of sole. L$, D$, Italian restaurant.

Tía Questa
Roberto Montesinos, Manager
8009 Norfolk Ave.
Bethesda, MD 20814
301-654-4443

Dishes cooked to order. Oil-free salad dressings, fresh fruit, poached snapper, oil-free and salt-free chips and salsa, enchiladas (request no oil), oil-free rice and beans. Call ahead for special orders. L$, D$, family Mexican restaurant.

ROCKVILLE

Paradise Restaurant
Peter Lee, Larry Chin, Managers
Congressional Shopping Plaza
176 Halpine Rd.
Rockville, MD 20852
301-770-0444

Dishes prepared to order upon request—ask for manager or owner. Steamed vegetables, green salad, wine vinegar. L$, D$$, family restaurant.

Raindancer Seafood House
Bill Scaggs, Jr., Manager
12224 Rockville Pike
Rockville, MD 20852
301-468-2300

Broiled or poached fish, chicken breasts, wine vinegar, salads, baked potatoes. Can handle special orders. L$, D$$, fine restaurant.

NEVADA

LAS VEGAS

Zachariah's
Golden Nugget Hotel
First & Fremont Sts.
Las Vegas, NV 89101
702-385-7111

See pages 119–120 for the restaurant's menu and discussion. B$, L$, D, fine restaurant.

NEW JERSEY

BRIDGEWATER

Main Street Restaurant
Anthony J. Bendetti, Manager
600 E. Main St.
Bridgewater, NJ 08807
201-526-1420

No reservations required. Largest salad bar in New Jersey. Features fresh fish, skinless chicken dishes, steamed vegetables. Open 7 days a week. L$, D$, fine restaurant.

LONG BRANCH

Harbor Island Spa
Jack Pfeffer, Manager
701 Ocean Ave.
Long Branch, NJ 07740
201-222-2600

Brown rice, steamed vegetables, raw vegetables, baked potatoes, oil-free dressing, fresh fruit, oatmeal, Wheatena. Chicken and fish prepared to order. B$$, L$$, D$$, fine restaurant.

MAPLEWOOD

Winolear Restaurant
Peter Pietz, Manager
5 Highland Place
Maplewood, NJ 07040
201-763-3083

Can cook to order. Pasta, tomato sauce, steamed vegetables, baked potatoes, salad bar, wine vinegar. Chicken to order. L$, D$$, family restaurant.

WEST ORANGE

40 Love
Monroe Krichman, Manager
622 Eagle Rock Ave.
West Orange, NJ 07052
201-376-8991

No advance notice necessary. Ask for manager in charge. Specializes in fresh fish. Salad bar. Can pressure cook fish and vegetables and sauté with nonstick frying pan on request. L$, D$, family restaurant.

NEW YORK

NEW YORK CITY

Akbar Restaurant
A. N. Malhotra, Manager
475 Park Ave.
New York, NY 10022
212-838-1717

No advance notice necessary. Chicken, fish, prawns—all baked on open fire in traditional clay oven, and can be cooked without salt or oil. Special curries and other dishes are made without oil or salt. L$, D$$, fine Indian restaurant.

Food Workshop
424 W. 43rd St.
New York, NY 10036
212-695-3602

Call at least 1 day ahead for special preparation and ask for Mr. Malik. L$, D$, fine restaurant.

The Garden of Eating
Marc Spiegel, Manager
1129 First Ave. at 62nd St.
New York, NY 10021
212-688-4949

Special dinners every night called "Cardio-Wise Dinners"—prepared with no salt, sugar, oil, or chemicals. The meals are complete: salad, brown rice, steamed vegetables, fish, and lemon and seltzer. All fruits are fresh. All vegetables are steamed or raw. L$, D$, fine restaurant.

Second location is:
212-02 Union Turnpike
Flushing, NY 11364
212-468-8483

Hisae's Restaurant
Mark A. Gerstein, Manager
45 E. 58th St.
New York, NY 10022
212-753-6555

All items cooked to order. Can accommodate any special requests to eliminate any oils or salt from dishes. No advance notice necessary. L$$, D$$, fine restaurant.

Janice's Fish Place
Linda Rubin, Manager
570 Hudson St.
New York, NY 10014
212-243-4212

No advance notice necessary. Steamed bass, steamed mussels in light tomato sauce, chicken with bean sprouts, poached salmon, poached cod, flounder with spinach and mushrooms, steamed lobster. Lightly blanched vegetables and brown rice with all dinners. D$$, fine restaurant.

Lincoln Square
Harry Silverstein, Manager
2 Lincoln Square
New York, NY 10025
212-799-4000

No advance notice necessary. Adds constantly to the variety of salad bar with changing seasons. B$, L$, D$, family restaurant.

O'Neal's 43rd
Michael Adams, Manager
147 W. 43rd St.
New York, NY 10036
212-869-4200

Baked potatoes, broiled or poached fish, pita bread, dinner salads, chicken breast cooked without skin. L$$, D$$, family restaurant.

R. Gross Vegetarian & Dairy
Abe Wexler, Manager
1372 Broadway
New York, NY 10018
212-921-1969

Special soup daily—no salt, no butter, no oil, no MSG. All fresh raw-vegetable salads; all fresh fruits; dry-curd cottage cheese; Shredded Wheat, Nutri-Grain, Wheatena cereals; hot fresh vegetable dinner; baked vegetable cutlet; baked salmon cutlet; broiled eggplant with onions and green peppers; chopped cold eggplant salad. Order pasta dishes in advance. B$, L$, D$, fine kosher restaurant.

Salta in Bocca
Fulvio Tramontina, Manager
179 Madison Ave.
New York, NY 10016
212-882-5243

When making reservations, mention that you are on the Pritikin diet. Upon request: vegetables can be steamed, can sauté in broth, marinara sauce without oil, skinned chicken breast. D$$, fine Northern Italian restaurant.

Tre Scalini
Giovanni De Saverio, Manager
230 E. 58th St.
New York, NY 10022
212-688-6888

No advance notice necessary. Food is prepared *à la carte* according to customer direction. Steamed vegetables, poached or broiled fish, skinned chicken, salads, whole-wheat pasta. L$$, D$$, fine Italian restaurant.

PENNSYLVANIA

ARDMORE

Hu-Nan Restaurant
Dr. E-Ni Foo, Manager
47 E. Lancaster Ave.
Ardmore, PA 19003
215-642-3050

No advance notice necessary. Ask for Betty. Most dishes can be prepared Pritikin-style. L$, D$, fine Chinese restaurant.

Saladalley
Amy Potterfield, Manager
Suburban Square
Ardmore, PA 19003
215-642-0602

Salad bar offers over 30 varieties of fresh vegetables and fruits. In lieu of salt, season with a wide variety of herbs and spices. Salad bar carries wine vinegar and spices. Special sandwich called the "Idler"—pita bread filled with your choice of chicken, tuna, or vegetables. L$, D$, family vegetarian self-service restaurant.

DOWNINGTOWN

Daniel's
John Fernando, Manager
Tabas Hotel
Downingtown, PA 19335
215-269-6000

Call ahead for special preparation. Fresh seafood (sole, flounder, etc.) à la Véronique, niçoise. Poulet aux champignons, broiled chicken with ginger, breast of chicken orientale. L$, D$$, fine restaurant.

NARBERTH

Governor's Over the Rainbow
Debbie Governor, Manager
856 Montgomery Ave.
Narberth, PA 19072
215-664-8589

Specializes in fresh fish, chicken, and very unusual pasta dishes. All fish, and some chicken and pasta entrées can be prepared Pritikin-style. Homemade soups for Pritikinites are fresh vegetable and Cuban black bean. No advance notice is required. Everything is available to go. Two Pritikin-guideline desserts on the menu. L$, D$, fine restaurant.

PHILADELPHIA

Eastern Chinese Restaurant
Chester Fung, Manager
8925 Krestown Rd.
Philadelphia, PA 19115
215-673-4646

All meals prepared steamed or boiled without any oil, salt, sugar, or MSG. Uses garlic and pepper. Major ingredients are fresh vegetables such as celery, onion, broccoli, snow peas, carrots, water chestnuts, bamboo shoots, mushrooms, bean sprouts, bok choy (Chinese celery), and bean curd. Fish filets also available. No need to call in advance. Popular dishes are sliced chicken with mixed vegetables with ginger sauce, smashed corn soup with bean curd. L$, D$, Chinese restaurant.

Hu-Nan Restaurant
E-Hsin Foo, Manager
1721 Chestnut St.
Philadelphia, PA 19103
215-567-5757

Items for Pritikin diners. No advance notice necessary. Makes own chicken stock and uses to steam or poach all vegetables and chicken. Fresh spices and herbs. L$, D$, Chinese restaurant.

John Wanamaker
Roberta Brown, Manager
Cottman Ave. & Roosevelt Blvd.
Philadelphia, PA 19149
215-331-5500, ext. 344

No advance notice necessary. Special vegetable sandwich prepared on pita bread with fresh zucchini, green pepper, onions, mushrooms, and tomatoes (ask waiter to hold the cheeses). Extensive salad bar—$2.99. Baked potatoes. Can sauté in broth. Can broil fish. Banquet facilities. L$, D$, family restaurant. Other locations in Pennsylvania.

King's Chinese Restaurant
Christopher Lee, Albert Lee, Managers
109 N. 10th St.
Philadelphia, PA 19107
215-928-9310

No advance notice is necessary. Inform waiter or waitress that food must be prepared in accordance with the Pritikin diet. L$, D$, Chinese restaurant.

Mayflower Restaurant
Donald Tang, Manager
1010 Cherry St.
Philadelphia, PA 19107
215-923-4202

Offers various fish, chicken, and vegetable entrées cooked for Pritikin diners. Brown rice available. L$, D$, Chinese restaurant.

Pastamania, Inc.
Ariel Keinan, Alfonso Man, Managers
7729 Castor Ave.
Philadelphia, PA 19152
215-342-1090

All items made on premises, including whole-wheat bread. Also features retail sale of items such as whole-wheat pasta (regular, tomato, or spinach), ravioli, manicotti, lasagna, quiches (mushroom or chicken) for home preparation. Mainly takeout service. Call for special party orders. L$, D$, Italian restaurant.

Riverfront Restaurant
Howard J. Wurzak, Manager
Delaware Ave. at Poplar St.
Philadelphia, PA 19123
215-925-7000

Vegetable salad bar, baked potatoes, broiled or poached fish, steamed vegetables, marinara sauce, sourdough bread, pita bread, whole-wheat bread, dinner salads, chicken breast cooked without skin. Can sauté in broth. L$, D$$, fine family restaurant.

Saladalley
Andrew Owen, Manager
4040 Locust St.
Philadelphia, PA 19104
215-349-7644

Salad bar offers over 30 varieties of fresh vegetables and fruits. In lieu of salt, season with a wide variety of herbs and spices. Salad bar carries wine vinegar and spices. Special sandwich called the "Idler"—pita bread filled with your choice of chicken, tuna, or vegetables. L$, D$, family vegetarian self-service restaurant.

Other locations:

Anthony DeMuro, Manager
1720 Sansome St.
Philadelphia, PA 19103
215-564-0767

Karen Berryman, Manager
The Bourse Bldg.
21 S. 5th St.
Philadelphia, PA 19104
215-627-2406

Siv'as
Amar Bhalla, Manager
34 S. Front St.
Philadelphia, PA 19106
215-925-2700

Call ahead for special preparation. Has been preparing special dishes for Pritikin diners for 3 years. Poultry, fish, and many vegetarian dishes. L$, D$, fine North Indian cuisine.

South East Chinese Restaurant
Raymond Fung, Manager
1000 Arch St.
Philadelphia, PA 19104
215-629-1888

Cuisine easily adapted to requirements of the Pritikin Program without sacrificing the flavor and uniqueness of Chinese food. No salt, sugar, oil, or MSG. Advance notice usually not required. Address questions and comments to Raymond or Anita. L$, D$, Chinese restaurant.

Super Natural
Mark Rhodes, Manager
1543 Spring Garden St.
Philadelphia, PA 19130
215-563-5338

International daily-changing menu includes steamed potato-stuffers (using about a dozen fresh vegetables), tofu dishes, whole-wheat spinach lasagna, fresh fish dishes. Large selection of the freshest of garden, fruit, and other healthful salads. L$, D$, family vegetarian fast-food restaurant.

Wildflowers
Ken Barnett, Manager
514 S. 5th St.
Philadelphia, PA 19147
215-923-6708

No advance notice necessary. Call ahead for any extra-special request, e.g., special dishes or fruits or celebration menus. Voted best salad buffet in USA, 1982, by 400 of the nation's leading restaurant critics. Most items can be prepared to satisfy Pritikin diet needs. L$$, D$$, fine restaurant.

SPRINGFIELD

John Wanamaker
Greg Poletti, Manager
1200 Baltimore Pike
Springfield, PA 19064
215-328-1000, ext. 344

No advance notice necessary. Special vegetable sandwich prepared on pita bread with fresh zucchini, green pepper, onions, mushrooms, and tomatoes (ask waiter to hold the cheeses). Extensive salad bar—$2.99. Baked potatoes. Can sauté in broth. Can broil fish. Banquet facilities. L$, D$, family restaurant. Other locations in Pennsylvania.

WILLOW GROVE PARK

Saladalley
Fran Kneisc, Manager
2500 Moreland Rd.
Willow Grove, PA 19090
215-659-1565

Salad bar offers over 30 varieties of fresh vegetables and fruits. In lieu of salt, season with a wide variety of herbs and spices. Salad bar carries wine vinegar and spices. Special sandwich called the "Idler"—pita bread filled with your choice of chicken, tuna, or vegetables. L$, D$, family vegetarian self-service restaurant.

TEXAS

ADDISON

Charley's Seafood Grill of Addison
David Schwandt, Manager
5348 Belt Line Rd.
Addison, TX 75340
214-934-8501

Ask for charbroiled fish prepared "dry," or request fish to be poached in water only. Salads, baked potatoes. L$, D$$, family restaurant.

AUSTIN

Captain Boomer's Restaurant
Charlie G. Candelas, Manager
12602 Research Blvd.
Austin, TX 78769
512-258-8888

No reservations required. Casual atmosphere. Fresh fish daily, fresh vegetable and fruit salad bar. D$$, fine restaurant.

Souper Salad Franchises
14 locations in Austin, Dallas,
Houston, TX; LaFayette, LA; and
Atlanta, GA
713-660-8952

Fresh, uncooked, unseasoned, untreated vegetables on 60-item salad bar. Iceberg and romaine lettuce, spinach, carrots, celery, radishes, cucumbers, yellow squash, zucchini, broccoli, cauliflower, cherry tomatoes, mushrooms, green peppers, red onions, and alfalfa sprouts. L$, D$, chain restaurant.

Yunnan Dynasty
Tom Swiss, Manager
2900 Anderson Lane
Austin, TX 78757
512-454-6677

Vegetable dishes include eggplant with garlic sauce, spicy bean curd, bamboo dishes with black mushrooms. Chicken dishes include chicken with pineapple, lemon chicken, chicken with bean sprouts. L$, D$, Chinese restaurant.

DALLAS

Lettuce Works
Cary Cooper, Manager
5984 W. Northwest Hwy.
Dallas, TX 75225
214-368-5211

Salad bar with over 40 items. All produce brought in fresh daily. Homemade soups. L$, D$, family vegetarian self-service restaurant.

Souper Salad Franchises
14 locations in Dallas, Austin, and
Houston, TX; LaFayette, LA; and
Atlanta, GA

Fresh, uncooked, unseasoned, untreated vegetables on 60-item salad bar. Iceberg and romaine lettuce, spinach, carrots, celery, radishes, cucumbers, yellow squash, zucchini, broccoli, cauliflower, cherry tomatoes, mushrooms, green peppers, red onions, and alfalfa sprouts. L$, D$, chain restaurant.

Vincent's Seafoods
Ann K. Marsh, Manager
13327 Midway Rd.
Dallas, TX 75234
214-387-3690

All special requests accommodated with no advance notice, including dry broiling, steaming, poaching; no salt. Baked potatoes, dinner salad. Family-owned restaurant with locations in the Dallas/Fort Worth area. L$, D$$, fine restaurant.

HOUSTON

Chancellor's Racquet Club
Forrest Jordan, Manager
6535 Dumfries
Houston, TX 77096
713-772-9955

Roast Cornish hen with orange sauce, Pritikin-style (1-day notice needed). Call and ask for Norma or Cassandra for special items. Selection of fish, skinned chicken, and vegetable dishes. Vegetable and fruit salad bars, breads, pasta. L$, D$$, family restaurant.

Le Depart Restaurant
Patricia Simpson, Manager
1717 Post Oak Blvd.
Houston, TX 77056
713-960-1888

No advance notice necessary. Poached snapper, grilled flounder, carpaccio, steamed vegetables. L$$, D$$, fine restaurant.

Souper Salad Franchises
14 locations in Houston, Austin,
Dallas, TX; LaFayette, LA; and
Atlanta, GA

Fresh, uncooked, unseasoned, untreated vegetables on 60-item salad bar. Iceberg and romaine lettuce, spinach, carrots, celery, radishes, cucumbers, yellow squash, zucchini, broccoli, cauliflower, cherry tomatoes, mushrooms, green peppers, red onions, and alfalfa sprouts. L$, D$, chain restaurant.

Tony's
Tony Vallone, Manager
1801 Post Oak Blvd.
Houston, TX 77056
713-622-6778

Always eager to follow any Pritikin menu and/or program. "Making the necessary substitutions for the Pritikin regimen is no problem whatsoever." L$$, D$$, fine restaurant.

SAN ANTONIO

Gini's Home Cooking
Gini & Tol Crowley, Managers
7214 Blanco
San Antonio, TX 78216
512-342-2768

No advance notice necessary. Fresh vegetable soup daily (fat-free, sugar-free), fresh vegetables daily, baked corn tostadas (oil-free), herb teas. L$, D$, family restaurant.

VIRGINIA

FAIRFAX

Chinese Gourmet
Domingo Guingab, Manager
9444 Arlington Blvd.
Route 50
Fairfax, VA 22031
703-591-8380

No advance notice necessary. Dishes cooked to order upon request. L$, D$$, Chinese restaurant.

WASHINGTON

SEATTLE

Rosellini's Four-10
Victor Rosellini, Manager
4th & Wall Sts.
Seattle, WA 98121
206-624-5464

Call ahead for special preparations. Baked potatoes, broiled or poached fish, steamed vegetables, marinara sauce, sourdough bread, whole-wheat pasta with notice, Pritikin minestrone soup, takeout deli. Any waiter will help with your request for special preparation. L$$, D$$, fine restaurant.

WASHINGTON, D.C.

Alfio's La Trattoria
Emanuel Koroulakis, Manager
5100 Wisconsin Ave., N.W.
Washington, DC 20016
202-966-0091

Salad bar, baked potatoes, broiled or poached fish, steamed vegetables, marinara sauce, dinner salads, oil-free salad dressing, chicken breast. Can sauté in broth. Call ahead for special orders. Reservations required. L$, D$$, fine Italian restaurant.

Hilda's Restaurant
Hilda Iber Hutchings, Manager
5125 MacArthur Blvd., N.W.
Washington, DC 20016
202-244-9191

Broiled or poached fish, steamed vegetables, dinner salads, oil-free salad dressings. Can sauté in broth. Will make chicken breast on request. Call ahead for special orders. Reservations required. L$, D$$, fine international cuisine.

Mel Krupin's
Mel Krupin, Manager
1120 Connecticut Ave., N.W.
Washington, DC 20036
202-331-7000

Reservations required. Call ahead for special orders. Baked potatoes, broiled or poached fish, steamed vegetables, marinara sauce, pita bread, dinner salads, wine vinegar, chicken breast. Can sauté in broth. L$, D$$, fine American restaurant.

Appendix

Optimal Dietary Recommendations: A Public-Health Responsibility

NATHAN PRITIKIN

*D*egenerative diseases, such as diabetes, heart disease, hypertension, and breast and colon cancer, are still widely assumed by many to be a natural part of getting older as the body "degenerates." If this is true, we are confronted with explaining why these diseases are essentially limited to the most developed and, theoretically, the most scientifically advanced populations in the world. In my view, these conditions are not diseases, but symptoms of chronic metabolic injury resulting from the highly processed, artificial diet eaten in developed areas, principally from the excessive amounts of cholesterol and fat consumed.

A toxin is any substance which when taken in excess can cause death. Cyanide, present in lima beans, is rarely reported as the cause of adverse effects when consumed in this food. It can be assumed that the amount of cyanide in lima beans is far below the toxic level. In contrast to cyanide, iron is necessary to maintain life; but even so, excess iron intake

Source: *Preventive Medicine,* Vol. 11 (1982), pp. 733–739. Reprinted by permission of Academic Press, Inc.

can cause iron overload of the liver and result in death. In Africa, among the Bantus, the use of iron pots furnishes three to five times as much iron as the amount specified in the United States Recommended Dietary Allowances (RDA). In these days of megavitamins, this may not seem much, but the excess reaches a toxic level creating iron overload of the liver in 75% of the males and 25% of the females, resulting in unnecessary deaths.

In the amounts in which they are consumed in Western countries, cholesterol and fat reach toxic levels. It is this toxicity that I hold responsible for the degenerative diseases—pathological processes resulting from aberrations in the intake and metabolic processing of lipid and cholesterol.

In 1955, when my cholesterol level hovered around 300 mg/dl, fueled by my daily ingestion of 700 mg of cholesterol, physicians assured me that it was in the high normal range, that my diet was excellent, and that stress and heredity were my principal heart-disease risk factors. Nevertheless, I soon developed coronary insufficiency so advanced that I was advised to completely limit all exercise. In retrospect, this circumstance might have been fortunate, saving me from a possible infarct resulting from the vigorous tennis matches in which I engaged at the time.

For 20 years prior, I had been closely following the epidemiology of cardiovascular and other degenerative diseases in the medical literature, though I had not been applying this information to my own lifestyle. I had concluded that atherosclerosis is essentially nonexistent in populations with adult cholesterol levels below 150 mg/dl. A feature common to all these populations seemed to be a cholesterol intake of less than 100 mg a day.

During the late 1940s and early 1950s, Keys reported the findings of over 25 investigations: without exception, he found heart disease to be rare in these low-cholesterol–consuming populations (11). Of particular interest were Keys's analyses of populations—especially the Japanese—who lost their immunity to heart disease when they migrated to areas in which cholesterol and fat intake were higher, and adopted the new diet.

The Japanese are heavy smokers, yet this well-established heart-disease risk factor seems to be of significantly less importance in the presence of a low-cholesterol and low-fat diet. Although they are number one among the developed nations in salt intake, hypertension, and strokes, the Japanese incidence of heart disease is the lowest among the developed nations. A 10%-fat diet keeps the average cholesterol level of this population at 150 mg/dl.

In the United States, where the mean population cholesterol level exceeds 200 mg/dl, both smoking and hypertension substantially contribute to the development of heart disease. Perhaps the low Japanese cholesterol levels are protective against the development of atherosclerosis in spite of these risk factors.

Among the populations that seem immune from heart disease is one close to our southern borders. Fifty thousand Tarahumara Indians, living in the isolation of the Sierra Madre Occidental Mountains in northern Mexico, are part of a natural dietary experiment that has been going on for the past 2,000 years. Their athletic stamina, as indicated by the ability to run up to 200 miles, has attracted the attention of a number of scientists. One of them, William E. Connor, has conducted a number of investigations of their diet and general health. He found no evidence of deaths from cardiovascular disease and concluded that their diet is typical of other populations among which heart disease is virtually nonexistent. Of their total caloric intake, fat comprises 10% (P/S = 2.0); protein, 13%; and carbohydrates, 75–80%. The diet provides 15–20 g/day of crude fiber, only 75 mg/day of cholesterol, and meets all nutritional requirements. Adult cholesterol levels among the Tarahumaras range from 100–140 mg/dl (5, 6).

In 1955, when I decided to change my high-cholesterol, high-fat dietary lifestyle, I adopted a diet nutritionally identical to the Tarahumara and other similar diets, though I endeavored to prepare the food in a manner pleasing to my Western-trained tastes. This is the same diet I have been recommending for 25 years, although for those with cholesterol levels of 250 mg/dl or greater, I found it was more effective to limit cholesterol intake to 15 mg a day, until serum levels dropped below 140 mg/dl.

In less than 3 years on this type of diet, my cholesterol level dropped to 100 mg/dl and it has remained in that range for 25 years. In the last 6 years, my dietary recommendations have been incorporated into the nutritional service at the Longevity Centers, and cholesterol levels there, on an average, drop 27% in 3–4 weeks.

Serum cholesterol levels of people who come to the Longevity Centers—mostly white Americans—drop quickly on a diet nutritionally similar to the Tarahumara diet: conversely, when Tarahumaras are given American intakes of cholesterol, serum cholesterol rapidly rises toward American levels (12). The response seems universal.

Framingham data early indicated that "normal" cholesterol levels in the U.S. were only normal for a country where heart disease is rampant. Even the early Cleveland Clinic angiographic data (14) destroyed the "normal" cholesterol level concept. Among 723 men, 17 to 39 years old, significant (>50%) coronary lesions were found to be directly related to cholesterol level even within the "acceptable" limits of serum cholesterol (Table 1).

TABLE 1

Significant Coronary Lesions Associated with Serum Cholesterol Levels (14)

Serum cholesterol (mg/dl)	Significant lesions (>50%) Percentage of total cases
<200	20
201–225	38
226–250	48
251–275	60
276–300	77

This growing mass of epidemiological evidence—all pointing in the same direction—was further illuminated by the findings of Brown and Goldstein, who were able to show the mechanisms involved in setting the safe limits of circulating serum cholesterol. To quote Michael Brown, "Why, therefore, is Western man oversaturating his receptors and depositing LDL cholesterol in his arteries?" To lower plasma levels of LDL (to ideal levels) requires a diet of less than 100 mg of cholesterol daily and thus excludes all meat products and eggs, "a diet which I would never eat, which allows almost nothing except nuts and berries" (4). I phoned Dr. Brown and said, "I have bad news for you—nuts are not on my diet—too high in fat. All that's left are berries." It did not take long to explain that the marvelous recipes adapted from American and foreign cuisines would give him a wide-ranging fare free from the risks of high-cholesterol and high-fat intake. The question that arises is why is there such reluctance to change the atherogenic diet?

Henry Blackburn wrote a splendid article (3), "The Public Health View of Diet and Mass Hyperlipidemia," whose thesis can be summarized in three sentences: "Atherosclerotic CHD is a public health phenomenon of affluent cultures. Population comparisons suggest that mass hyperlipidemia is a prime requisite for mass atherosclerosis. On the basis of available evidence, the habitual diet of a culture is, in turn, the chief factor leading to hyperlipidemia." Blackburn divides the world into four categories according to cholesterol levels, as shown in Table 2.

TABLE 2
Relationship of Mean Population Cholesterol Level and Incidence of Atherosclerosis (3)

Mean population cholesterol level (mg/dl)	Incidence of atherosclerosis
120	Rare
160	Minimal
190	Reduced
220–280	Epidemic

He selects a mean population cholesterol level of 160 mg/dl as the best compromise (minimal CHD, and good palatability), and states, "Population total cholesterol averages above 200 mg/dl are found incompatible with optimal cardiovascular health for populations." Other expert groups have concurred with this general position. The American Health Foundation Conference on "Health Effects of Blood Lipids: Optimal Distributions for Populations" made an optimal recommendation of 160 mg/dl (16).

But what Blackburn recommends to the U.S. public with its average serum cholesterol of 220 mg/dl is the American Heart Association (AHA) diet: 30% fat and 300 mg cholesterol, because, he points out, large-scale studies have shown it is able to produce cholesterol drops of 6–7%. A quick calculation indicates that a 7% drop from 220 mg/dl still leaves those hapless individuals with excessively high levels of 205 mg/dl, which Blackburn himself stated is incompatible with optimal cardiovascular health. To achieve the ideal, a mean population cholesterol level of 160 mg/dl, requires a drop of 27%. On my recommended diet, this 27% cholesterol reduction occurs in a month (8).

The hopelessness of the position of those who cannot see beyond the AHA diet is apparent, also, in a statement made by AHA spokesman Scott Grundy that the AHA diet could only reduce the mean cholesterol level of U.S. men to 200 mg/dl. He goes on to say: "Yet despite such a change, half the male population would have cholesterol concentrations over 200 mg/dl. Many workers believe that levels over 200 mg/dl are still too high for adequate prevention of atherosclerotic disease. Thus, it is doubtful that atherosclerotic disease in our society can be obliterated by diet control alone, and additional measures will have to be taken to rid the American population of this disease. The methods are currently not available and will have to be developed through new research" (9).

The conclusion that diet alone cannot reduce the mean serum cholesterol level below 200 mg/dl is true with the AHA diet, of course. But Grundy asserts that this 30%-fat, 300-mg cholesterol diet is the most effective diet for lowering cholesterol level—which is not true. Since the AHA diet does not work, he blames this on "genetics" and says new methods not currently available will have to be developed through new research.

While health professionals knowledgeable about the dietary basis of CHD are unable to face up to the magnitude of the dietary changes that must be made to achieve adequate lowering of serum cholesterol, they are willing to use hypocholesteremic drugs that have been discredited because of the possible excess cancer risk they introduce, to subject hyperlipidemic patients to an ileal bypass that will reduce cholesterol level little more effectively than a diet with less than 10% fat and 100 mg of cholesterol, and to continue to make dietary recommendations of 300 mg cholesterol and 30% fat when during 20 years of trials this diet has failed to reduce cholesterol levels adequately.

Worse yet, it should be noted that these dietary recommendations when first made to the nation in 1961 had not been adequately tested. Pearce and Dayton, who directed the 8-year Wadsworth Veterans Administration AHA diet trial with 846 men, commented, "It is important to remember that no population under study has been consuming a diet high in polyunsaturated fats over long periods of time" (15). After the Wadsworth study, Dayton not only said that he would not recommend a high-polyunsaturated (PUFA) diet to most of his patients, but that a diet of 10% fat would be his choice. In the official report the investigator wrote, "The diet tested in this program was selected for purely pragmatic reasons: we did not believe we could mount and sustain a trial of any other type of lipid-lowering diet in this institution. Epidemiological studies favor the conclusion that a low-fat diet is perhaps the promising path to longevity" (7).

Though high-PUFA diets fail to reduce the risk of heart disease, they may *enhance* the risk of cancer. The 1982 National Academy of Sciences report, "Diet, Nutrition, and Cancer," concluded that a relationship between fat and cancer was most persuasive (13). T. C. Campbell, one of the authors of the report, stated that if a diet is high in PUFA, total fat should be less than 20% of total calories because of the possible increased cancer risk. So convinced is Campbell of the danger of excess fat, that he stated, "The relationship between diet and cancer, in my opinion, is now more persuasively established than the one between diet and heart disease" (10).

What, then, was the recommendation that flowed from this observation? Campbell continued, "We decided to come up with a reasonable, practical number, something the whole population might work toward. So we recommended a reduction in fat intake from a current 40% of total calories to 30%, although I would suggest getting it down to about 20%. In China, where I was in June, it's only 9%. So you can go down to 20% and not experience problems."

But the public recommendation is 30%! Cancer and heart-disease researchers are alike in their tendency to treat the public as though they were incapable of accepting an optimal dietary recommendation.

My experience with 10,000 people who have been through my centers and millions who have read or heard about my diet belies this underestimation of a large part of the public. Why shouldn't everyone who wishes to follow an optimal diet be informed of the facts and be encouraged to make the necessary lifestyle changes?

When people achieve rapid health improvements, as very many do on an optimal diet, they become motivated to continue permanently so as to maximize health gains and avoid regressing. My diet, combined with exercise, has been effective not only with patients with cardiovascular symptoms but with noninsulin-dependent diabetics, 75% of whom are off insulin in 4 weeks, including some who have been taking it for 20 years (2). In 4 weeks, 85% of hypertensives on drug therapy are off medication, with normal blood pressure, on this same diet-exercise regimen. In 3 weeks, cholesterol and triglycerides drop 25–30% on the regimen. Compliance, considering the difficulties in pursuing this kind of dietary lifestyle in a milieu in which not even health authorities encourage it, is surprisingly good: over a 5-year period, compliance varies between 50–75% (1).

If health-care authorities recommended that cholesterol intake not exceed 100 mg/day and fat intake not exceed 10% of total calories, the benefits experienced by those who follow my program could be experienced by millions more. The benefits would extend not only to sick people; healthy active people would also gain. Many world-class athletes are on my diet and are experiencing thrilling new, higher levels of performance. In the October 9, 1982, Triathlon in Hawaii, five of these athletes will have been identified as being on the Pritikin diet.* It is encouraging from a public health viewpoint that all of these athletes adopted the new dietary lifestyle from reading my books or by word of mouth. I became aware of them only when I was contacted by one of their group. The event is grueling, consisting of a 2½-mile ocean swim, a 112-mile bicycle race, and a 26-mile marathon run, all in continuous sequence.

The experts, already in agreement on the biochemical goals, are now beginning to agree on the guidelines: cholesterol intake needs to be under 100 mg/day and fat intake not over 10%. Leading investigators—Seymour Dayton in CHD, T. C. Campbell in cancer, and J. W. Anderson in diabetes—all are looking respectfully at the 10%-fat diet, or are already using it.

New health recommendations from authoritative sources are also moving slowly in the direction of advocating optimal fat and cholesterol intakes. These are encouraging trends, but there are still many problems to be overcome in terms of facilitating widespread enactment of these dietary goals. Only by replacing "compromise" by "ideal" can we ever hope to achieve the optimal diet for maximum quality and duration of life.

REFERENCES

1. Barnard, R. J., Guzy, P. M., Rosenberg, J. M., and O'Brien, L. T. Effects of an intensive exercise and nutrition program on patients with coronary artery disease: 5-year follow-up (Abstract). *Med. Sci. Sports Exercise* 14, 179 (1982).
2. Barnard, R. J., Lattimore, L., Holly, R. G., Cherny, S. and Pritikin, N. Response of noninsulin-dependent diabetic patients to an intensive program of diet and exercise. *Diabetes Care* 5, 370–374 (1982).

---

*Of a field of 850 athletes, those on the Pritikin diet came in first, second, and fourth, setting a new course record of 9 hours, 8 minutes. The first place winner has been on the diet for 4 years. The third place winner, who was not identified as being on the Pritikin diet, is a younger brother of the athlete placing second. Since the contest started 4 years ago, with the exception of the Pritikin winners, only four other athletes have completed the race in under 10 hours.

3. Blackburn, H. The public health view of diet and mass hyperlipidemia. *Cardiovasc. Rev. Rep.* Aug. 1980, 433–442; Sept. 1980, 361–369.

4. Carpenter, M. "Healthy" receptors can't handle even "normal" lipid. *Med. Tribune* 21, 3, 19 (1980).

5. Cerqueira, M. T., Fry, M. M. and Connor, W. E. The food and nutrient intakes of the Tarahumara Indians of Mexico. *Amer. J. Clin. Nutr.* 32, 905–915 (1979).

6. Connor, W. E., Cerqueira, M. T., Connor, R. W., Wallace, R. B., *et al.* The plasma lipids, lipoproteins, and diet of the Tarahumara Indians of Mexico. *Amer. J. Clin. Nutr.* 31, 1131–1142 (1978).

7. Dayton, S., Pearce, M. L., Hashimoto, S., Dixon, W. J. and Tomiyusau, U. A controlled clinical trial of a diet high in unsaturated fat in preventing complications of atherosclerosis. *Circulation* 40, Suppl. 2, 1–63 (1969).

8. Diehl, H., and Mannerberg, D. Hypertension, hyperlipidaemia, angina, and coronary heart disease, *in* "Western Diseases: Their Emergence and Prevention" (H. C. Trowell and D. P. Burkitt, Eds.), p. 400. Harvard Univ. Press, Cambridge, 1981.

9. Grundy, S. M. Saturated fats and coronary heart disease, *in* "Nutrition and the Killer Diseases" (M. Winick, Ed.), p. 76. Wiley, New York, 1981.

10. In the war against cancer the latest weapons are fruits and vegetables. *People* July 12, 1982, 65–68.

11. Keys, A., Kimura, N. Kusukawa, A., Bronte-Stewart, B., *et al.* Lessons from serum cholesterol studies in Japan, Hawaii, and Los Angeles. *Ann. Int. Med.* 48, 83–94 (1958).

12. McMurry, M. P., Connor, W. E., and Cerqueira, M. T. Dietary cholesterol and the plasma lipids and lipoproteins in the Tarahumara Indians: A people habituated to a low cholesterol diet after weaning. *Amer. J. Clin. Nutr.* 35, 741–744 (1982).

13. National Research Council. Committee on Diet, Nutrition and Cancer. "Diet, Nutrition, and Cancer," pp. 5–20, 5–21. National Acad. Sci. Washington, D.C., 1982.

14. Page, I. H., Berrettoni, J. M., Butkas, A., and Sones, F. M. Prediction of coronary heart disease based on clinical suspicion, age, total cholesterol and triglyceride. *Circulation* 62, 625–645 (1970).

15. Pearce, M. L. and Dayton, S. Incidence of cancer in men on a diet high in polyunsaturated fat. *Lancet* 1, 464–467 (1971).

16. Wissler, R. W., Armstrong, M., Bilheimer, D. *et al.* Conference on the health effects of blood lipids: Optimal distributions for populations. *Prev. Med.* 8, 715–732 (1979).

Restaurant Evaluation Response Form

Please let us know about your dining experiences at the restaurants we have listed in Chapter 8.

Your name (optional) _____

Name of restaurant _____

Name of restaurant manager (if known) _____

Address _____

Telephone number _____

Page number on which restaurant is described _____

Type of food you ordered _____

_____

Comments _____

_____

_____

_____

_____

_____

_____

_____

Comments (con'd) _____

_____

_____

_____

_____

_____

_____

_____

_____

_____

_____

_____

_____

_____

_____

_____

_____

_____

_____

_____

_____

Restaurant Evaluation Response Form

Please let us know about your dining experiences at the restaurants we have listed in Chapter 8.

Your name (optional) _____

Name of restaurant _____

Name of restaurant manager (if known) _____

Address _____

Telephone number _____

Page number on which restaurant is described _____

Type of food you ordered _____

_____

Comments _____

_____

_____

_____

_____

_____

_____

_____

Comments (con'd) _____

_____

_____

_____

_____

_____

_____

_____

_____

_____

_____

_____

_____

_____

_____

_____

_____

_____

_____

New Restaurant Suggestion Form

Undoubtedly, many of you will be visiting restaurants in cities other than those we have included and will be discovering new dining experiences in locales already represented. If you have had successful dining experiences at restaurants that have served you in accordance with what you think the Pritikin guidelines to be, we would like to know about it.

Use these forms to send us the basic information, and we will contact the restaurants. Thank you for your participation.

Restaurant _____

Name of owner (if known) _____

Name of manager (if known) _____

Address (please give zip code) _____

_____

Telephone number _____

Type of food served _____

Price range _____

Your comments _____

_____

_____

_____

_____

_____

_____

Comments (con'd) _____
_____
_____
_____
_____
_____
_____
_____
_____
_____
_____
_____
_____
_____
_____
_____
_____
_____
_____
_____
_____
_____

New Restaurant Suggestion Form

Undoubtedly, many of you will be visiting restaurants in cities other than those we have included and will be discovering new dining experiences in locales already represented. If you have had successful dining experiences at restaurants that have served you in accordance with what you think the Pritikin guidelines to be, we would like to know about it.

Use these forms to send us the basic information, and we will contact the restaurants. Thank you for your participation.

Restaurant _____

Name of owner (if known) _____

Name of manager (if known) _____

Address (please give zip code) _____

_____

Telephone number _____

Type of food served _____

Price range _____

Your comments _____

_____

_____

_____

_____

_____

Comments (con'd) _____

_____

_____

_____

_____

_____

_____

_____

_____

_____

_____

_____

_____

_____

_____

_____

_____

_____

_____

_____

_____

Special Services Available

The reader may request information on the following.
(Please send a self-addressed, stamped envelope.)

- Nutrition and diets for people of all ages and activity levels.
- Availability of Pritikin foods in your area.
- In-residence 13-day and 26-day medically supervised East and West Coast centers. These programs are ideal for people who are taking medication or have a weight problem. You learn a new way of life and feel the benefits while you are there. The majority of individuals taking medication find that after 2 to 4 weeks at a Pritikin center, they no longer require their drugs. Five-year follow-up studies indicate that very few return to their medication.
- In-residence one-week Educational Center located in Maui, Hawaii, designed for those who do not require medical supervision. Learn the Pritikin lifestyle and enjoy the Pritikin cuisine in a vacation setting.

Physicians and other health professionals may request:

- Scientific evidence of the effects of the Pritikin diet on various diseases.
- Reprints of any of our published studies.
- Copies of unpublished studies.
- Printed diet guides for your patients.

You may also request that your name be added to our mailing list so that new information can be sent to you as it becomes available. Write:

Pritikin Programs
P.O. Box 5335
Santa Barbara, CA 93108

Index